A grammar of Azeri

The language of Azerbaijan

Dr Yavar Dehghani

Preface

This book grows out of a PhD thesis completed at the School of Linguistics, Faculty of Humanities and Social Sciences, La Trobe University, Melbourne, Australia, in May 1998. The original thesis took a comparative approach, examining and contrasting the grammatical structures of four languages: Azeri, Turkish, English, and Persian. A condensed version of that comparative work was later published as a book by Lincom Europa, a publisher specialising in linguistics and language science.

Azeri — also known as Azerbaijani — is a Turkic language spoken by tens of millions of people, primarily in Azerbaijan, a country situated at the crossroads of Eastern Europe and Western Asia, as well as in the northwestern regions of Iran, where a substantial Azeri-speaking population has lived for centuries. As a member of the Turkic language family, Azeri is closely related to Turkish and shares a number of structural features with it, while also having developed its own distinct grammatical characteristics over time. It is one of the major languages of the wider Caucasus region and holds official status in the Republic of Azerbaijan.

The present book, however, takes a different focus from the original thesis. Rather than comparing Azeri with other languages, it zooms in on Azeri grammar alone, exploring it in depth and on its own terms. It is worth noting that this book deals exclusively with grammar and does not cover Azeri phonology — that is, the sound system of the language — which would require a separate and dedicated treatment.

For readers who are new to the study of languages, it may be helpful to know that grammar and phonology are two distinct areas of linguistics. Grammar concerns the rules and structures that govern how words are formed and how sentences are put together, while phonology deals with the sounds of a language and how they function. This book is concerned entirely with the former.

Table of Contents

Abbreviations

Introduction

Linguistic family

The dialects of Azeri

Language family tree

1 Morphology

1.1 Introduction

1.2 Derivational suffixes

1.2.1 Class changing derivational suffixes

1.2.2 Class maintaining derivational suffixes

1.2.3 Other suffixes

1.2.4 Rarely used derivational suffixes

1.2.5 Borrowed derivational affixes

1.3 Inflectional suffixes

1.3.1 Inflectional suffixes for nouns

1.3.1.1 Case suffixes

1.3.1.2 Possessive and genitive suffix

1.3.1.3 Person/Number suffixes

1.3.2 Inflectional suffixes for verbs

1.3.2.1 Tense suffixes

1.3.2.2 Aspect suffixes

1.3.2.3 Mood suffixes

1.3.2.4 Participial and relativising suffixes

1.3.2.5 Causative suffixes

1.3.2.6 Other inflectional suffixes

1.3.3 The suffixed copular construction

1.4 The phrasal or lexical nature of nominal suffixes

1.5 The distinction between derivational and inflectional verbal suffixes

1.6
1.7 Compounding
1.7.1 Compounding in Persian
1.8 Reduplication
1.8.1 Reduplication of nouns and adjectives
1.8.2 Reduplication of verbs
1.8.2.1 Reduplication of verb in the subjunctive mood
1.8.3 Reduplication of the first syllable of adjectives

2 Syntax of simple clauses
2.1 Introduction
2.2 Constituent order
2.2.1 Basic sentence types in Azeri

2.2.2 Constituent order in embedded clauses
2.3 Case system in Azeri
2.3.1 Nominative case
2.3.2 Accusative case
2.3.3 Dative case
2.3.4 Ablative case
2.3.5 Locative case
2.3.6 Instrumental case
2.3.7 Benefactive case
2.4 Pronouns, reflexives, and reciprocals
2.4.1 Personal pronouns
2.4.2 Reflexive pronoun
2.4.3 Reciprocal pronoun
2.4.4 Demonstrative pronouns
2.4.5 Indefinite pronouns
2.5 Passive construction
2.5.1 Introduction
2.5.2 Passivisation in simple clauses
2.5.3 Passive-like constructions
2.5.4 Passivisation out of complement clauses
2.5.5 Constraints on the passive construction
2.6 Copular construction
2.6.1 Existential constructions

2.6.2 Periphrastic constructions
2.6.3 Cleft clause constructions
2.7 Imperatives and optatives
2.7.1 Differences between 1st and 3rd person suffixes and 2nd person suffix
2.7.2 Constraints on imperatives in Azeri
2.8 Interrogative construction
2.8.1 Yes-no questions
2.8.2 WH-questions
2.9 Coordination
2.9.1 NP coordination
2.9.2 VP coordination
2.9.3 Other conjunctions

3 **Syntax of complex clauses**
3.1 Introduction
3.2 Causative constructions
3.2.1 Introduction
3.2.2 Morphological causatives
3.2.3 Syntactic causatives
3.2.4 Case assignment and the accessibility hierarchy
3.2.5 Constraints on causativisation
3.2.5.1 A constraint on the causativisation of ditransitive clauses
3.2.5.2 A constraint on the causativisation of lexical verbs
3.2.6 Double causatives
3.2.7 Causativisation of compound verbs
3.2.8 The interaction between causativisation and passivisation

3.3 Embedded clauses
3.1.1 Complement clauses
3.1.1.1 Infinitive complement clauses
3.1.1.2 Indicative complement clauses
3.1.1.3 Subjunctive complement clauses

3.1.1.4 Optative complement clauses
3.1.1.5 The *goy* construction
3.1.1.6 Properties of complement clauses
3.1.1.7 Constraints on the selection of complement clauses
3.3.2 Adjunct clauses
3.3.2.1 Adverbial clauses
3.3.2.2 Relative clause constructions
3.3.2.2.1 Head-final relative clause constructions
3.3.2.2.2 Head-initial relative clause constructions
3.3.2.2.3 Further properties of relativisation
3.3.2.2.4 Headless relative clauses

Abbreviations

A	Non high vowel
ABL	ablative
ACC	accusative
Adj	adjective
Ant	anterior
ASP	aspect
ATR	advanced tongue root
BEN	benefactive
C	consonant
CAUS	causative
COMP	complementiser
COND	conditional
CONJ	conjunction
Cons	consonantal
Cont	continuant
CONT	continuous
COP	copula
Cor	coronal
DAT	dative
DEF	definite
Del-Rel	delayed released
DO	direct object

EXI	existential
FUT	future
GEN	genitive
I	High vowel
ID	indirect object
IMP	imperative
INFI	infinitive
INST	instrumental
Lat	lateral
LOC	locative
N	noun
Nas	nasal
NEG	negative
NOM	nominative
NP	noun phrase
NPAST	non past tense
O	object
OPT	optative
P	Persian
PASS	passive
PAST	past tense

PL	plural
POSS	possessive
PRT	participial
Q	question
RECIP	reciprocal
REL	relativiser
S	subject
SG	singular
Son	sonorant
Strid	strident
SUBJ	subjunctive
Syll	syllabic
V	verb/vowel
VP	verb phrase
1	first person
2	second person
3	third person
[ ]	phonetic representation
/ /	phonological representation
+	morpheme boundary
⍰	zero
~	phonetic alternation
j	voiced palato-alveolar affricate
y	palatal glide

Introduction

Linguistic family

Azeri[1] is a member of the Turkic language group (see Figure 1.2) which itself is regarded as a subgroup of the Altaic family (Comrie, 1981; Katzner, 1986; Kornfilt, 1987). The Altaic languages are spoken over a territory extending from Turkey to the west, across ex-Soviet central Asia into Mongolia and China, and on to the Pacific Ocean. The genetic relation among Altaic family languages is not clear. The calssification within this language family varies and is controversial. One of these is the Micro-Altaic classification, which includes three branches within this family: Turkic, Mongolian, and Tugusic (Comrie, 1981:39).

The classification within Turkic branch itself is also complex. Turkic languages and dialects are close to each other and often mutually intelligible, and this makes it harder to draw a clear boundary among them. The main reason for the complexity of classification in this branch seems to be the continuous migration of Turkic people, which eventually has led to the mixing of these languages and their dialects with each other, or with other languages (Comrie, 1981:43; Kornfilt, 1987:620).

Currently, Azeri is spoken in Iran by about 15,000,000 people. Most Azeri speakers inhabit the four provinces in the northwestern parts of Iran, i.e. West Azerbaijan, East Azerbaijan, Ardabil and Zanjan (see Figure 1.1).

Azeri has been influenced heavily by Persian. A primary reason for this influence is that Persian and Azeri speakers have had the same nationality, religion and culture at least for twenty centuries. They have a common heritage which has been a result of interaction between Islam and Iran. Islam as the traditional religion of most Turkic speakers has resulted in the strong influence of Arabic and Persian on Turkic languages. (Comrie, 1981:47). Comrie states that Persian has had widespread influence on those Turkic languages and dialects that coexist with Iranian languages and dialects, for instance the Iranian dialects of Azeri with respect to phonology, morphology and syntax. As a result, Persian has influenced Azeri in almost every aspect except in case marking. Persian words constitute a considerable part of the Azeri speakers' vocabulary.

Persian is the official language in Iran. This language is spoken by about 23 million that is about 50 percent of the population in Iran (SBS World Guide, 1995:300). In Iran, Azeri, like Kurdish and Gilaki is regarded as a regional language, and is also referred to as "Torki", "Türki", and "Torki ye Azeri". It is considered a local language for mass media, e.g. local TV and radio programs, local newspapers and magazines.

In Grimes' ethnologue (1992:639), this language is called South Azerbaijani or Azeri, which is spoken by more than 20 percent of the population in Iran. According to Grimes, there are also some Azeri speakers in Afghanistan, Iraq, Syria, Turkey,

Azeri is occasionally written using Arabo-Persian script in Iran. In fact, Azeri has no formal orthography, and the script in which Azeri is written is the Persian script which itself is derived from a revised version of Arabic. Persian has been written in this script since the conquest of Islam in the seventh century A.D (Katzner, 1986:16). This type of orthography is not adequate for the language system of Azeri. It has a non-vocalised nature, and leads to multiple ambiguities in writing, as there are only characters for three vowels, i.e. /a/, /ä/, /u/ in this script. Thus, there is no character for other vowels, especially for /ü/, /ö/, /I/ which are different from Persian vowels. Therefore, reading and understanding the written form of Azeri is difficult for even those native speakers who are highly educated in Persian.

There are some classic versions of Azeri in the works of Nesimi (1369-1404) and of Fuzuli (d. 1555) (Asher, 1994: 291).

Azeri is also spoken in the Republic of Azerbaijan by about six million people (Katzner, 1986:123; SBS World Guide, 1995:40). It is suggested that there are distinct dialect differences between the Azerbaijani of the former USSR and Iranian Azeri in phonology, morphology and syntax (Grimes, 1992:639; Asher, 1994:291).

The dialects of Azeri

Grimes (1992) counts several dialects of Iranian Azeri based on their tribal diversity such as Aynallu, Karapapakh, Tabriz, and Afshar. However, since, in Iran, tribes have gradually been integrated in cities and towns, the dialect classification is no longer basedon tribal variation, and the dialects are distinguished based on four different Azeri speaking provinces: Tabrizi, Urumiyei, Zanjani, and Ardabili. Among these dialects, the Tabrizi dialect is regarded as the standard dialect. The reason is that this dialect is spoken by the majority of Azeri people, and it is the prestige dialect. Furthermore, most written Azeri is in this dialect, from literary prose and poems to local newspapers. These dialects are distinguished by phonological and lexical criteria but there is no syntactic difference among them. All the speakers of these dialects can understand each other effectively.

Language family tree

Altaic

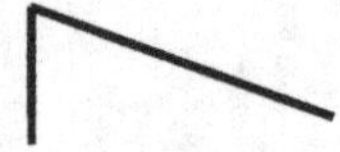

Mongolian Turkic Tungusic

Chuvash Kipchak Southern Turkic Eastern Turkic
Northern Turkic

South-Western Turkic Karlurlk
Eastern

HunnicOguz

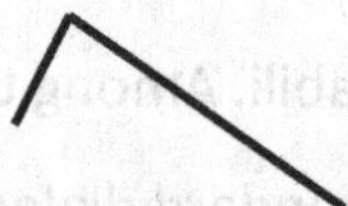

Turkish Azerbaijani

Northern Azerbaijani
Southern
Azerbaijani(Republic of Azerbaijan)
(Iranian
Azerbaijan)

Tabrizi Zanjani Urumiyei Ardabili

(This classification is partly based on Comrie, 1981)

Chapter 1 Morphology

Introduction

Azeri morphology is predominantly agglutinative and suffixing. Thus, all native affixes of Azeri are suffixes, and there is only one prefixing process where the first syllable of the adjective is prefixed via reduplication (see section 1.7.3). However, there are a few borrowed prefixes which are used infrequently (see section 1.2.5).

Because of vowel harmony, each suffix has either two or four phonetic forms based on backness and roundness harmony. In the following tables, we will mention the phonetic forms for each suffix. In this chapter, first we will discuss the derivational suffixes in Azeri. Then, we will introduce the inflectional suffixes.

1.1 Derivational suffixes

Derivational suffixes were very productive in older Azeri (i.e. about 50 years ago)[2]. Thus, there are a lot of words which have been constructed with these suffixes. But in modern Azeri, most of these suffixes have lost their productivity and in most cases borrowings are used instead of derived native words. In modern Azeri, because of the influence of an extended education in Persian and of radio and television (whose programs are in Persian), almost all of the derived words are being replaced by the borrowed words.

The concept of productivity is somehow ambiguous for Azeri derivational suffixes. The reason may be that most of these suffixes can be considered as productive diachronically, and as unproductive synchronically. That is, they could form new words in the past, and before the introduction of many borrowed words into the language. But these suffixes no longer form new words as a result of pre-emption by borrowed words.

Aronoff (1976:35) makes a distinction between productive and unproductive word- formation processes. In his view, those processes which still form neologisms are alive and therefore productive, and those processes which do not form neologisms are dead and unproductive. Matthews (1991:70) claims that a productive word-formation process must be able to create a potential lexeme.

Considering the above mentioned concepts for productivity, we will use the following criteria to distinguish between productive and unproductive suffixes in Azeri:

(a) if a suffix can still form new words in modern Azeri, it is productive; (b) if a suffix can form potential words whose meaning can be predicted easily, but it no longer forms new words, the suffix will be regarded as semi-productive; (c) if a suffix does not form new words and does not form potential words with a predictable meaning, it will be considered unproductive.

We can classify Azeri derivational suffixes into three groups based on whether or not they change the class of a stem: those which change the class of the stem; those which maintain the class of the stem and only change its meaning; and those which can be both class-changing and class-maintaining.

Beside native derivational suffixes, there are several borrowed ones which will be introduced later in this section. In the following tables, we will introduce each suffix with its phonetic forms, meaning and examples. For each productive suffix, we will provide six examples, and for unproductive ones, we will mention all known examples incurrent Azeri.

---

[2] From about 50 years ago, with the beginning of formal education in Persian and then with the gradual introduction of Persian radio and television programs, the number of borrowed words increased dramatically.

To represent derivational suffixes in a concise way, we will use]] notation. For example, the English suffix *ly* which changes an adjective to an adverb can be illustrated as follows, using this notation:] ly]

Adj Adv

Table 1.1 Class changing derivational suffixes

] Iš] V N [iš], [Iš], [üš], [uš] the process of the verb	/at/	'throw!'	/at-Iš/	'shooting'
	/dur/	'stand!'	/dur-uš/	'standing'
	/gäl/	'come!'	/gäl-iš/	'coming'
	/gül/	'laugh!'	/gül-üš/	'laughing'
] Ix] V Adj [ix], [Ix], [üx], [ux] having the quality of the verb	/ach/	'open!'	/ach-Ix/	'open'
	/bur/	'turn!'	/bur-ux/	'bending'
	/käs/	'cut!'	/käs-ix/	'minced'
	/sök/	'tear!'	/sök-üx/	'torn'
] lI] N Adj [li], [lI], [lü], [lu] having plenty of the quality specified by the noun	/dıl/	'tongue'	/dıl-lı/	'expressive'
	/Išlg/	'light'	/Išlg-lI/	'bright'
	/toz/	'dust'	/toz-lu/	'dirty'
	/üz/	'face'	/üz-lü/	'rude'
] mAlI][3] V Adj [mäli], [malI] having the potential quality of the verb; worthy of being Verbed	/gäz/	'stroll!'	/gäz-mäli/	'worthy of strolling'
	/get/	'go!'	/get-mäli/	'worthy of going'
	/gör/	'see!'	/gör-mäli/	'worthy of being seen'
	/ich/	'drink!'	/ich-mäli/	'worthy of being drunk'

] sIz]	/ad/	'name'	/ad-sIz/	'unknown'
N Adj	/ev/	'home'	/ev-siz/	'homeless'
[siz], [süz], [sIz], [suz]	/güj/	'power'	/güj-süz/	'powerless'
Privative	/pul/	'money'	/pul-suz/	'poor'

Table 1.2 Semi-productive derivational suffixes

] gI]	/at/	'throw!'	/at-gI/	'bullet'
V N	/bit/	'grow!'	/bit-gi/	'a grown thing'
[gi], [gI], [gü], [gu]	/bil/	'know!'	/bil-gi/	'knowledge'
something that is Verbed (under normal circumstances)	/chal/	'play (music)!'	/chal-gI/	'music'
	/ut/	'swallow!'	/ut-gu/[4]	'a swallowed thing'
] mAz][5]	/öl/	'die!'	/öl-mäz/	'long-living'
V Adj	/sol/	'fade!'	/sol-maz/	'unfading'
[mäz], [maz]	/say/	'pay attention!'	/say-maz/	'indifferent'
without the quality specified by the verb	/utan/	'be shy!'	/utan-maz/	'rude'

Table 1.3 Unproductive derivational suffixes

] Ar]	/ach/	'open!'	/ach-ar/	'key'
V N	/bax/	'look!'	/bax-ar/	'sight'
[är], [ar] agent of the quality specified by the verb; the process of the verb	/uch/	'fly!'	/uch-ar/	'bird'

] gAj] V N [g?äj], [gaj] agent of the verb in a restricted meaning, denoting instrument or tool	/dö/ /say/ /tut/ /üz/	'beat!' 'count!' 'catch!' 'swim!'	/dö-gäj/ /say-gaj/ /tut-gaj/ /üz-gäj/	'tool for pounding' 'counter' 'handle' 'swimmer'
] gAn] V Adj [gän], [gan] characterised by the quality specified by the verb	/allš/ /challš/ /oyna/ /sürüš/ /unut/	'catch fire!' 'move!' 'play!' 'slip!' 'forget!'	/allš-gan/ /challš-gan/ /oyna-gan/ /sürüš-gän/ /unut-gan/	'flammable' 'mobile' 'playful' 'slippery' 'forgetful'
] gIn] V Adj [gin], [gIn], [gün], [gun] having the quality specified by the verb to an ordinary degree	/bit/ /daš/ /još/ /yet/ /yor/	'grow!' 'overflow!' 'boil!' 'ripen!' 'make tired!'	/bit-gin/ /daš-gIn/ /još-gun/ /yet-gin/ /yor-gun/	'grown' 'overflowing' 'boiled' 'ripe' 'tired'
] IjI] V N [iji], [IjI] agent	/at/ /apar/ /örgän/ /sat/	'throw!' 'take!' 'learn!' 'sell!'	/at-IjI/ /apar-IjI/ /örgän-iji/ /sat-IjI/	'shooter' 'messenger' 'learner' 'seller'
] Im] V N [im], [Im] the action specified by the verb	/art/ /ax/ /bich/ /ich/	'increase!' 'flow!' 'harvest!' 'drink!'	/art-Im/ /ax-Im/ /bich-im/ /ich-im/	'increase' 'flowing' 'harvesting' 'drinking'

] Intl] V N [inti], [Intl], [üntü], [untu] something which has the quality specified by the verb	/ax/ 'flow!' /ax-Intl/ 'something which flows' /ov/ 'rub!' /ov-untu/ 'something which is rubbed' /tap/ 'find!' /tap-Intl/ 'something discovered' /tök/ 'pour!' /tök-üntü/ 'remains'
] mA] V N [mä], [ma] something which has the quality specified by the verb	/blla/ 'mix!' /blla-ma/ 'fresh milk' /dogra/ 'cut to pieces!' /dogra-ma/ 'a type of meal' /dondur/ 'freeze!' /dondur-ma/ 'ice cream' /govur/ 'fry!' /govur-ma/ 'fried meal' /toxu/ 'knit!' /toxu-ma/ 'textile'

1.2.2 **Class maintaining derivational suffixes**

Of the suffixes illustrated below, /chI/ is productive, /dAš/ is semi-productive, and /jIl/ is unproductive.

Table 1.4 Class maintaining derivational suffixes

] chI][6] N N [chi], [chI][7] occupation, agent	/ara/ 'middle' /ara-chI/ 'mediator' /ballx/ 'fish' /ballx-chI/ 'fisherman' /dämir/ 'iron' /dämir-chi/ 'blacksmith' /odun/ 'wood' /odun-chu/ 'wood cutter'
] dAš] N N [daš], [däš] someone who has the same condition or sharing the same	/ad/ 'name' /ad-daš/ 'someone with the same name as another' /jan/ 'body' /jan-daš/ 'someone intimate with another' 'friend' /yol/ 'way' /yol-

N with another person	daš/
] jIl] N N [jil], [jIl] someone who has the quality specified by N more than others	/baš/ 'head' /baš-jIl/ 'someone who is the head of others' /iš/ 'work' /iš-jil/ 'someone who works more than others'

1.2.3 **Other suffixes**

Three suffixes can change the class of words which they attach to. They also can maintain the class of some other words. These suffixes are as follows:

---

[6] This suffix is also affixed to borrowed words; for example, it can attach to the borrowed word, /šikar/ 'hunting' to form /šikar-chl/ 'hunter'.

llx: [lüx], [lux], [lix], [llx]. If this suffix attaches to noun stems, it forms a new noun with the meaning 'a quality, instrument, or a place for N'. Therefore, it is class-maintaining for the noun class, as the following illustrate:

/ot/	'grass'	/ot-lux/	'grass-plot'
/üz/	'face'	/üz-lüx/	'mask'
/ušax/	'child'	/ušax-llx/	'childhood'

When this suffix attaches to an adjective, it changes the adjective to a noun, meaning 'the quality specified by the adjective'. We can see this function in the following examples:

/gözäl/	'beautiful'	/gözäl-lix/	'beauty'
/pis/	'bad'	/pis-lix/	'badness'
/sag/	'alive'	/sag-llx/	'being alive'
/ujuz/	'cheap'	/ujuz-lux/	'cheapness'

Unlike most other suffixes, this suffix is still productive and its equivalent borrowed suffix /i/ is used rarely. It also affixes to borrowed words as in /gäda-llx/ 'begging'. In the past, it was very productive as a suffix denoting occupations as in /dišchi-lix/ 'dentistry', but in current times the borrowed suffix /i/ is used for such purposes.

yAjAx: [yajax], [yäjäx]. This suffix can attach to verb stems and form a noun with the meaning 'something which has the quality specified by the verb'. We can see this function of the suffix in the following examples:

/al/	'get!'	/al-yajax/	'claim'
/gäl/	'come!'	/gäl-yäjäx/	'future'
/gech/	'pass through!'	/gech-yäjäx/	'past'
/ver/	'give!'	/ver-yäjäx/	'debt'
/yan/	'burn!'	/yan-yajax/	'fuel'

This suffix is productive, and it is used in the formation of future time verbs (see section 1.1.3).

Ax: [ax], [äx]. This suffix can attach to verbs and construct a noun with the meaning 'something which has the quality of the verb, or a place for the quality of the verb', as shown below:

/boya/	'paint!'	/boya-ax/	'painting'
/gech/	'pass through!'	/gech-äx/	'passage'

It can also attach to verbs and form an adjective with the meaning 'having the quality of the verb'. This function of the suffix is illustrated in the following examples:

/gorx/	'be afraid!'	/gorx-ax/	'afraid'
/hürk/	'flee!'	/hürk-äx/	'cowardly'

This suffix is unproductive.

1.2.4 Rarely used derivational suffixes

There are several derivational suffixes which are not productive, and are currently used in very few words. These suffixes are listed in the following tables with an example for each of them:

Table 1.5 Rarely used derivational suffixes

Suffix	Example			
] Am] V N	/dogra/	'mince!'	/dogra-am/	'piece'
] gA] V N	/don/	'turn!'	/don-ga/	'bend'
]] V N	/olch/	'measure!'	/olch-u/	'scale'
] Ilg N] N	/damar/	'vein'	/damar-jlg/	'small vein'
] m] N Aj N	/dil/	'tongue'	/dil-maj/	'translator'
] sA] N n Adj	/ay/	'moon'	/ay-san/	'moon-like'

1.2.5 Borrowed derivational affixes

As mentioned, in current Azeri, most of the native derivational suffixes have become fossilised, in that, except for a few of them, most no longer function to form new words. One reason is the borrowing of a huge number of Persian words which reduces the need for derivational suffixes; furthermore, there are some borrowed prefixes and suffixes which function as a substitute for native suffixes. Some of these borrowed affixes can attach to both native and borrowed stems, and some others can only attach to borrowed stems. In the following tables, we will introduce those borrowed prefixes and suffixes which are used frequently in Azeri and which can attach to some native stems.

There are only two frequently used borrowed prefixes. They are illustrated in the following table:

Table 1.6 Borrowed derivational prefixes

[ba [	/ädäb/	'politeness'	/ba-ädäb/	'polite'
Adj N	/iman/	'faith'	/ba-iman/	'faithful'
having the quality	/savad/	'literacy'	/ba-savad/	'literate'
specified by the noun	/täjrübä/	'experience'	/ba-täjrübä/	'experienced'
[bi [	/ädäb/	'politeness'	/bi-ädäb/	'impolite'
Adj N	/kar/	'work'	/bi-kar/	'unemployed'
privative	/pul/	'money'	/bi-pul/	'poor'

These two prefixes function as equivalents for the native suffixes /sIz/ and /lI/ respectively, for example, /bi-pul/ = /pul-suz/, and /ba-ädäb/ = /ädäb-li/.

There are several borrowed suffixes in Azeri. In the following table the more frequently used borrowed suffixes are illustrated:

Table 1.7 Borrowed derivational suffixes

] ban] N N a person who guards or maintains N as his usual occupation	/bag/ /jängäl/	'garden' 'forest'	/bag-ban/ /jängäl-ban/	'gardener' 'forester'
] baz] N N the person whose occupation involves N	/gumar/ /guš/	'gambling' 'bird'	/gumar-baz/ /guš-baz/	'gambler' 'bird keeper'
] chA] N N diminutive	/bag/ /käläk/	'garden' 'boat'	/bag-cha/ /käläk-chä/	'small garden' 'small boat'
] dan] N N standard container for N	/gänd/ /gül/	'sugar' 'flower'	/gänd-dan/ /gül-dan/	'sugar-bowl' 'flower-pot'
] dar] N N the person who owns N	/el/ /pul/	'tribe' 'money'	/el-dar/ /pul-dar/	'the head of tribe' 'rich'
] i] N Adj pertaining to N; having the quality of N	/bazar/ /tarix/	'market' 'history'	/bazar-i/ /tarix-i/	'commercial' 'historical'
] istan] N N a place designed to contain N	/gäbir/ /gül/	'grave' 'flower'	/gäbir-istan/ /gül-üstan/	'cemetery' 'rose-garden'
] saz] N N the person who is the maker or repairer of N as his usual occupation	/chirag/ /sahat/	'lamp' 'watch'	/chirag-saz/ /sahat-saz/	'lamp-maker' 'watch-maker'

The possibility of considering the above words as compounds was explored because like compounds (see section 1.6), they do not have vowel harmony. However, since the stresspattern in these words is similar to that of other words rather than compounds, we can regard them as an stem plus a suffix. In other words, the stress in compounds is on the left-most component, as in /�gIrmIzI-badIm��an/ 'tomato', while it is on the right-most syllable in the above words, as in /balIx-�chI/ 'fisherman'.

Therefore, it seems that besides compounds, borrowed suffixes also do not necessarily follow vowel harmony in Azeri.

Inflectional suffixes

As mentioned in section 1.1, every suffix has more than one phonetic form due to vowel harmony. All of these are regular. In the following tables we will introduce every inflectional suffix with its phonetic forms. First, the inflections for nouns will be introduced, and the relevant template will be suggested. Then, after introducing the template for verbs, their inflections will be discussed. The copular construction will be mentioned in a separate section.

1.1.1 Inflectional suffixes for nouns

Azeri nouns are inflected for case and number.

1.1.1.1 Case suffixes

There are eight cases in Azeri. The case system of Azeri is nominative-accusative. The case marker for nominative case is zero. Since the genitive case has a special behaviour, it will be discussed separately in section 1.1.1.1. We can see the remaining suffixes in thefollowing table:

Table 1.8 Case suffixes

Accusative suffix		
I:9 [i], [I], [ü], [u]	/äl-i/ /at-I/ /göz-ü/ /gol-u/	(cf. /äl/ 'hand') (cf. /at/ 'horse') (cf. /göz/ 'eye') (cf. /gol/ 'arm')
Dative suffixyA: [yä], [ya]	/äl-yä/ /at-ya/	(cf. /äl/ 'hand') (cf. /at/ 'horse')
Ablative suffix dAn: [dän], [dan]	/ev-dän/ /bag-dan/	(cf. /ev/ 'home') (cf. /bag/ 'garden')
Locative suffix		
dA: [dä], [da]	/ev-dä/ /bag-da/	(cf. /ev/ 'home') (cf. /bag/ 'garden')
Benefactive suffix IchIn: [ichin], [IchIn], [üchün], [uchun]	/äl-ichin/ /at-IchIn/ /göz-üchün/ /gol-uchun/	(cf. /äl/ 'hand') (cf. /at/ 'horse') (cf. /göz/ 'eye') (cf. /gol/ 'arm')
Instrumental suffix InAn: [inän], [Inan], [ünän], [unan]	/äl-inän/ /at-Inan/ /göz-ünän/ /gol-unan/	(cf. /äl/ 'hand') (cf. /at/ 'horse') (cf. /göz/ 'eye') (cf. /gol/ 'arm')

As we observe in the above table, the dative suffix is underlyingly considered as /yA/. However, on the surface, this suffix has two alternants: the form with the glide [yA], following stems ending in a vowel, and the form without the glide, [A], which follows stems ending in a consonant, as illustrated below:

	Stem	Dative
	-------	--------
'bee'	[arl]	[arlya]
'black'	[gara]	[garlya][10]
'dog'	[it]	[itä]
'garden'	[bag]	[baga]

It seems that a reasonable approach to this alternation is to propose a glide deletion rule which deletes the glide after the final consonant of the stem, as illustrated below:

[y] ? ? / C + ——

which can be written in terms of distinctive features as follows:

[Syll] ? ? / [+Cons] + ——

-Cons

[10] The final low vowel of the stem is raised based on the raising rule (see section 2.5.2.6).

Since there is no direct phonological evidence to motivate this rule, and it can only be motivated by morphological forms, it is discussed in this chapter, rather than in the phonology chapter. Some indirect evidence in favour of this rule comes from Table 2.7 where there is no consonant cluster at a morpheme boundary having /y/ as its second consonant.

Beside the dative case suffix, there are other inflectional suffixes like participial, subjunctive, and first person copula which have the same alternation in the surface forms and this rule also applies to them[11].

1.1.1.2 Possessive and Genitive suffixes

To indicate a possession relation, the possessor takes a genitive case, while the possessedentity takes a possessive suffix:

1 Ali -nin kitab -I

Ali -GEN.3SG book -POSS.3SG

'Ali's book.'

The possessive suffix is inflected for person and number and involves agreement between possessor and possessed. For example in *Häsän-in äl-i* 'Hasan's hand', a suffix is affixedto the possessed /äl/ agreeing with the possessor, *Häsän*. The suffix /i/ is here affixed to the possessed to agree with the third person singular, *Häsän*. We can see this agreement for person and number in the following:

/män-im äl-im/	'my hand'	/biz-im äl-imiz/	'our hand'
/sän-in äl-in/	'your hand'	/siz-in äl-iz/	'your (PL) hand'
/o-nun äl-i/12	'his hand'	/olar-In äl-lär-i/	'their hand'

In the above examples, the genitive case /Im/ for the first person possessors is the same for both singular and plural (as in /män-im and /biz-im/). But the suffix for possessed entities is different. It is /Im/ in the singular (as in /äl-im/), and /ImIz/ in the plural (as in

/äl-imiz/). Here, we can say that /Im/ is the first person singular suffix, and there is a separate suffix, /Iz/, which is added to this suffix, and forms the first-person plural (as in

/äl-im/, /älimiz/).

The genitive suffix /In/ for the second person possessors is also the same in the singular and plural (as in /sän-in/, and /siz-in/), while the suffix for possessed entities is different. The singular suffix is /In/ as in /äl-in/ and the plural suffix /Iz/ as in /äl-iz/.

For the third person, the genitive suffix for singular and plural possessors is also the same, namely /In/[13]. However, in the plural, the number suffix /lar/ occurs before this suffix as in /o-lar-In/. The suffix for third person possessed entities is also the same for the singular and plural. Once again in the plural, the suffix /lar/ occurs before this suffix (as in /äl-i/ and /äl-lär-i/). The following tables illustrates the possessive nad genitive suffixes.

Table 1.9 Possessive suffixes[14]

		/äl/ 'hand'	/at/ 'horse'	/göz/ 'eye'	/gol/, 'arm'
1SG	Im	/äl-im/	/at-Im/	/göz-üm/	/gol-um/
2SG	In	/äl-in/	/at-In/	/göz-ün/	/gol-un/
3SG	I[15]	/äl-i/	/at-I/	/göz-ü/	/gol-u/
1PL	ImIz	/äl-imiz/	/at-ImIz/	/göz-ümüz/	/gol-umuz/
2PL	Iz	/äl-iz/	/at-Iz/	/göz-üz/	/gol-uz/
3PL	lArI	/äl-läri/	/at-larI/	/göz-läri/	/gol-larI/

Table 1.10 Genitive case suffixes

1SG	Im	/män-im/ 'my'
2SG	In	/sän-in/ 'your'
3SG	In	/o-nun/ 'his'
1PL	Im	/biz-im/ 'our'
2PL	In	/siz-in/ 'your' (PL)
3PL	In	/olar-In/ 'their'

Apart from some phonological changes, no other process takes place when the possessive and case suffixes are combined. We can see the co-occurrence of the Possessive and Accusative suffixes in the following examples:

/män-im äl-im-i/ 'my hand-ACC'

/sän-in äl-in-i/ 'your hand-ACC'

/o-nun äl-in-i/ 'his/her/its hand-ACC'

/biz-im äl-imiz-i/ 'our hand-ACC'

/siz-in äl-iz-i/ 'your (PL) hand-ACC'

/olar-In äl-in-i/ 'their hand-ACC'

Other case forms occur in the same order as that of the accusative case, e.g. /äl-im-dä/,

/äl-im-yä/, /äl-im-inän/, /äl-im-ichin/, and /äl-im-dän/.

In the case of recursive possessive constructions, there is also regularity in affixing the suffixes to the possessor and the possessed. Consider the following examples:

/män-im gardaš-Im/ 'my brother'
/män-im gardaš-Im-In äl-i/ 'my brother's hand'

As we see, the first construction, that is /män-im gardaš-Im/, is regarded as a single possessor, and then the genitive suffix for the third person singular (corresponding to

/gardaš/) is affixed to it. Finally, the suffix for entities possessed by third person singular

possessors are affixed to the possessed entity, namely /äl/.

Blake (1994:152-153) states that in many languages, the possessive affix cross-references the possessor, but in Turkish, there is a genitive affixed to the possessor. This is also true in Azeri where the possessor always takes a genitive suffix, and both the genitive and possessive suffixes are necessary, as shown by the following examples:

2 (a) glz -In sach -I
girl -GEN.3SG hair -POSS.3SG
'the girl's hair'

(b) * glz girl sac h hair -I - POSS.3SG

(c) * glz -In sach girl - GEN.3SG hair

In Azeri, it is possible to delete the genitive suffix in a possessive relation to make a compound noun (see section 1.6 for this type of compounding process):

3 (a) ušag -In paltar -I

child -GEN.3SG clothes -POSS.3SG

'the child's clothes'

(b) ušag paltar -I

child clothes -POSS.3SG

'children's clothes'

It is possible for the possessed entity in a possession relation to become a possessor. In this case, a genitive suffix for the third person is affixed to the possessed entity which already has a possessive suffix. Then, the new possessed entity takes a possessive suffix,as illustrated below:

4 (a)	män	-im	gardaš	-Im
	I	-GEN.1SG	brother	-POSS.1SG

'my brother'

(b)	män	-im	gardaš	-Im	-In	kitab	-I
	I	-GEN.1SG	brother	-POSS.1SG	-GEN.3SG	book	-POSS.3SG

'my brother's book'

As shown in (4a), /gardaš/ 'brother' which is the possessed entity and has the possessive suffix, /Im/, takes the genitive suffix for the third person singular, i.e. /In/ and becomes a possessor as in (4b), and the new possessed entity, i.e. /kitab/ 'book' takes the possessive suffix, /I/.

When the possessive constituent, e.g. /kitab/ 'book' in (4b) occurs within a sentence, it always takes another case suffix which is affixed to the possessed entity following the possessive suffix:

5 Ali -nin kitab -In -I oxu -du -m
Ali -GEN.3SG book -POSS.3SG -
ACC read -PAST -1SG'I read Ali's book.'

1.1.1.3 Person/Number suffixes

There is a regular plural suffix for all nouns in Azeri, namely /lAr/, as illustrated by the following examples:

/äl/	'hand'	/äl-lär/	'hands'
/at/	'horse'	/at-lar/	'horses'

There is an ambiguity involving the third person possessors. Consider the following data:

(a)	/äl-lär-im/	'my hands'	(b)	/äl-lär-imiz/	'our hands'
(c)	/äl-im/	'my hand'	(d)	/äl-imiz/	'our hand'
(e)	/äl-lär-i/	'his hands'	(f)	/äl-lär-i/	'their hands'
(g)	/äl-i/	'his hand'	(h)	/äl-lär-i/	'their hand'

As we can see in (a-d), there is a distinction between first person singular and plural, and also between singular and plural nouns. However, there is no distinction among 'his hands', 'their hands', and 'their hand' as illustrated by (e), (f), and (h). The following reasons may account for such a three-way ambiguity:

(a) Since the third person plural suffix, /lAr/, and the nominal plural suffix, /lAr/, are homophonous in the surface form of /äl-lär-i/, we cannot determine whether /lAr/ is the plural suffix for the noun as in 'his hands', or it is the person/number suffix as in 'their hand'.

(b) When these two suffixes co-occur in the underlying forms, only one of them surfaces.Thus, the underlying form for (f) is /äl-lär-lär-i/, whereas the underlying form for (h) is /äl-lär-i/.

At this point, we can suggest a template for nominal inflectional suffixes as follows:

Table 1.11The template for nominal inflectional suffixes

Stem	Number	Possessive	Case
äl ba š dil gö z Häsän	lä r lä r	in imiz	dä lna ni dä n in

In the above template, first the number suffix is affixed to the stem, then the possessive, and finally one of the case suffixes is affixed to the noun. When the noun is a possessor, the number suffix is only followed by the genitive case.

1.1.2 Inflectional suffixes for verbs

Here, we suggest the following template for verbal inflectional suffixes which we discussone by one in the sections that follow:

Table 1.12The template for verbal inflectional suffixes[16]

Root	Valency changing suffixes (Passive, Causative) 17	Negative suffix	Mood suffixes	Continuous aspect suffix	Perfect aspect suffix	Tense suffix	Person/ Number suffixes

ge y ga l ver	dir il	mä mä		Ir	miš	di d I d i	lä r m m
du r gät ir gal			a s ä			dI	lä r la r

1.1.2.1 **Tense suffixes**

There are two tenses in Azeri. The past tense is marked by the suffix /dI/, contrasting with the non-past which is indicated by the absence of /dI/, i.e. by a zero morpheme. There are three possibilities for using the past tense suffix: it can occur alone after the verb root; it can occur after the perfect aspect suffix; and it can occur after the continuous suffix, yielding a past continuous verb. Some examples follow:

/gal/	'stay!'	/gal-dI/	'he stayed'
/gal-mIš-dI/	'he had stayed'	/gal-Ir-dI/	'he was staying'

Future time forms in Azeri involve the copular construction which will be dealt with in section 1.1.1.

1.1.2.2 **Aspect suffixes**

There are two aspect suffixes in Azeri: one for the continuous aspect and another for the perfect aspect. There is a constraint on the non past tense suffix; it can not occur withoutan aspect suffix. For example, /galIr/ 'he stays' includes the continuous suffix /Ir/ plus a non past tense morpheme which surfaces as zero. These suffixes are shown in the following table:

Continuous aspect	Ir: [ir], [Ir], [ür], [ur]	/gal-Ir-dIm/ /ver-ir-dim/	'I was staying' 'I was giving'
Perfect aspect	mIš: [miš], [mIš], [müš], [muš]	/gal-mIš-dIm/ /ver-miš-dim/	'I had stayed' 'I had given'

The reason for assigning two different slots to aspect suffixes is that they can co-occur asin /gal-Ir-mIš-dIm/ 'I had been staying' where the continuous aspect suffix precedes the other.

1.1.2.3 Mood suffixes

There are four additional suffixes for the conditional, imperative, optative andsubjunctive moods, as in the following table:

Conditional mood	sA: [sä], [sa]	/gal-sa/ /ver-sä/ /gal-sa-	'if he stays' 'if he gives'

		dI/ /ver-sä-di/	'if he stayed' 'if he gave'
Imperative mood	2SG	?	/gal/	'stay!'
	2PL	yIz: [yiz], [yIz][18] [yüz], [yuz]	/gäl-yiz/ /gal-yIz/ /gül-yüz/ /dur-yuz/	'come!' (PL) 'stay!' (PL) 'laugh!' (PL) 'stand!' (PL)
Optative mood	1SG	yIm: [yim], [yIm] [yüm], [yum]	/gäl-yim/ /gal-yIm/ /gül-yüm/ /dur-yum/	'I (may) come.' 'I (may) stay.' 'I (may) laugh.' 'I (may) stand.'
	1PL	yAx: [yäx], [yax]	/gäl-yäx/ /gal-yax/	'We (may) come.' 'We (may) stay.
	3SG	sIn: [sin], [sIn]	/gal-sIn/ /ver-sin/	'He (may) stay.' 'He (may) give.'
	3PL	sInIAr: [sinlär], [sInlar]	/gal-sInlar/ /ver-sinlar/	'They (may) stay.' 'They (may) give.'
Subjunctive mood		yA: [yä], [ya]	/gal-ya/ /ver-yä/ /gal-ya-dI/ /ver-yä-di/	'he may stay' 'he may give' 'he might stay' 'he might give'

The subjunctive suffix, /yA/, occurs in subjunctive complement clauses (see section 3.1.1.3). It can also occur in simple sentences, where it always co-occurs with an auxiliary like /šayäd/, as in:

6 o šayäd gäl -yä
3SG (NOM) may come -SUBJ.3SG

'He may come (possibly).'

This suffix can be concatenated with the continuous aspect suffix, /Ir/, and surface as

/yAr/ which conveys habituality. For example, the sentence /här gün evyä gälyär/ means 'he comes home everyday'. In the past tense, it means 'used to' or 'would' as in /o evyä gälyärdi/ 'he would come home' or 'he used to come home'. This suffix can also conveycertainty concerning the action specified by the verb. For example, /galyaram/ means that'I will certainly stay'.

One piece of evidence to support this analysis is that the continuous aspect suffix can not occur after /yAr/ as we see in the ungrammaticality of */gal-yar-Ir/ (cf. /gal/ 'stay!'). This shows that the continuous suffix already exists there. Note that /yA/ + /Ir/ surfacing as

/yAr/ is consistent with what we know about Azeri phonology, since one of the two adjacent vowels at morpheme boundaries is deleted.

Corroborating evidence shows that /yAr/ like the continuous aspect suffix can occur before the perfect suffix, /mIš/, as in: /gal-yar-mIš/, 'He had been staying.', whereas the subjunctive suffix, /yA/ can not, as in: * /gal-ya-mIš/

The conditional mood suffix, /sA/, co-occurs with /yAr/ in conditional sentences to construct the antecedent and consequent parts of the sentence, respectively. They are illustrated in the following conditional sentence:

7	o	gäl	-sä	män	get	-yä	-ir	-äm
	3SG (NOM)	come	-COND	I	go	-SUBJ	-CONT	-1SG

'It he comes, I will go.'

The imperative mood suffix for the second person singular surfaces as zero. Therefore, the base form of the verb in Azeri is in the imperative form as in /get/ 'go!'. The imperative suffix for the second person plural is /yIz/ which is affixed to the base form ofthe verb, as in /getyiz/ 'you (PL) go!'.

The optative suffix is inflected for person and number. The verb in this mood denotes a

suggestion or desire made by the speaker, as in: /biz getyäx/, 'It is better for us to go'.

1.1.2.4 **Participial and relativising suffixes**

Participial I	yenjA: [yenjä], [yenja]	/gal-yenja/ 'as soon as one stays' /ver-yenjä/ 'as soon as one gives'

Participial II	yAn: [yän], [yan]	/gal-yan/ 'staying, who is staying' /ver-yan/ 'giving, who is giving'
Relativising	dIg: [dig], [dIg], [düg], [dug]	/gal-dIg-Im/ 'where I stayed' /ver-dig-im/ 'which I gave' /dur-dug-um/ 'where I stood' /gör-düg-üm/ 'which I saw'

The first participial suffix, /yenjA/, is shown in the following sentence:

8 sän gäl -yenjä män get -di -m
2SG (NOM) come -PRT I go -
PAST -1SG 'I went as soon as you came.'

It is affixed to the verb in the first clause of the sentence and shows that the action specified by the verb has taken place immediately before that of the verb in the other clause.

We can see an example of the second participial suffix, /yAn/, in the following sentence:

9 män gäl -yän kiši -ni tanI -
Ir -am I
come -PRT man -ACC know -CONT -
1SG 'I know the man who is coming.'

This suffix can also co-occur with the locative suffix, /dA/, affixed to the verb in the first clause of the sentence. It shows the co-occurrence of the actions specified by the two verbs, as illustrated by the following sentence:

10 sän gäl -yän -dä män get -di
-m 2SG come -PRT -LOC I go -
PAST -1SG 'When you came, I went.'

Since, here, this suffix occurs preceding another suffix, i.e. /dA/, it is considered as a participial; otherwise, it functions as a relativising suffix (see section 3.1.2.2).

The relativising suffix, /dIg/, can occur in sentences such as the following:

11 män gör -düg -üm kiši get -di
I see -REL -POSS.1SG man go -PAST.3SG

'The man whom I saw went.'

This suffix forms a relative clause, and always occurs before the possessive form (see section 3.1.2.2).

The slot for the participial suffixes in the template for verbs is after the slot for the negative suffix. There can not be any other suffix preceding or following a participial suffix, except for the locative suffix which can occur after the participial /yAn/. Thus, the possible word form with a participial suffix will be as follows:

Stem + (passive/causative) + (negative) + participial + (locative)

The slot for the relativising suffix will involve the nominal template, where this suffix occurs after the stem and before the number suffix, as in:

Stem + Relativiser + Number + (Possessive) + (Case)

1.1.2.5 **Causative suffixes**

The causative suffix surfaces as one of the following three allomorphs:

I /Irt/ which is affixed only to those stems ending in an affricate[19], as in:

/uch-urt/ 'Make someone fly.'

/ich-irt/ 'Make someone drink it.'

/gach-Irt/ 'Make someone run.'

/gech-irt/ 'Make someone pass.'

II /dIr/ which is affixed to the stems ending in other consonants, as shown in the following:

/al-dIr/ 'Make someone buy it.'

/gazan-dIr/ 'Make someone earn it.'

/utan-dIr/ 'Make someone be ashamed of it.'

/yaz-dIr/ 'Make someone write it.'

III /t/ which is affixed to the stems ending in a vowel, as in the following:

/elä-t/ 'Make someone do it.'

/goza-t/ 'Make someone raise it.'

/toxu-t/ 'Make someone knit it.'

/yala-t/ 'Make someone lick it.'

Few lexical exceptions have been found, which take a different suffix, as illustrated below:

/gop-art/ 'Make someone disconnect.'

/gorx-ut/ 'Make someone scared.'

/yey-dirt/ 'Make someone eat it.'

1.1.2.6 **Other inflectional suffixes**

Infinitive suffix	mAx: [mäx], [max]	/gal-max/ /ver-mäx/	'to stay' 'to give'
Negative suffix	mA: [mä], [ma]	/gal-ma/ /ver-mä/	'do not stay' 'do not give'
Passive suffix	Il: [il], [Il], [ül], [ul]	/poz-ul/ /sat-Il/ /söy-ül/ /ver-il/	'be erased' 'be sold' 'be loved' 'be given'

The slot for the infinitive suffix in the template is the same as that of the relativising suffix, namely after valency changing suffixes, the negative, and before the number suffix. Thus, the possible verb form with the infinitive suffix will be as follows (see section 5.1.2.2 for the relevant examples):

stem + (passive/causative) + (negative) + infinitive + (number) + (possessive) + (case)

1.1.3 The suffixed copular construction

Besides noun and verb suffixes, there is a copular suffix whose function is different from that of others. This suffix is inflected for tense, person and number. It involves two different paradigms, one for the past and one for the non past, as follows:

Non past			
tense 1SG	yA	1P	yIx
2SG	m	L	sIz
3SG	sA	2P	dIIA
	n	L	r
	dI	3P L	
Past tense			
1SG	IdIm	1PL	IdIx
2SG	IdIn	2PL	IdIz
3SG	IdI	3PL	IdIIAr

This suffix can be affixed to nouns, adjectives, adverbs, and also to nouns in the locative case to form copular constructions. We can see these functions of the suffix in the following examples:

	Non past		Past
	----------		-------
/ag/ 'white'	/ag-yam/	'I am white.'	/ag-IdIm/'I was white.'
/evdä/ 'at home'	/evdä-yäm/	'I am at home.'	/evdä-idim/[20] 'I was at home.'
/tänbäl/'lazy'	/tänbäl-yäm/	'I am lazy.'	/tänbäl-idim/ 'I was lazy.'
/ušag/ 'child'	/ušag-yam/	'I am a child.'	/ušag-IdIm/ 'I was a child.'

One important function of the copular suffix is to form the future tense construction, where first the derivational suffix, /yAjAx/, is affixed to verb, and then the copular suffixis affixed to the output. Some examples follow:

/gal/	'stay!'	/gal-yajax-am/	'I am going to stay.'
/ver/	'give!'	/ver-yäjäx-äm/	'I am going to give.'

Note further that examples like:

/gal-yajax-IdIm/ (cf. /gal/ 'stay!') 'I was going to stay.'

can be analysed as exhibiting the past tense together with prospective aspect.

The third person copular suffix, i.e. /dI/ can be deleted from the clause when it is preceded by /yAjAx/, as in [gal-ajax-(dI)] 'he will stay'. In Turkish, the deletion of copula takes place generally for all non past suffixes, and it seems that in Azeri, /yAjAx/ has motivated the start of such deletion process.

Another suffix, /ImIš/, can co-occur with /yAjAx/ in the copular construction. We can see an example in the following sentence:

/gal/ 'stay!' /gal-yajax-ImIš-IdIm/[21] 'I was supposed to stay.'

The suffix /ImIš/ is different from the perfect aspect suffix /mIš/ in function and meaning.

The former is affixed to nouns, adjectives, and to the derived nouns ending in /yAjAx/. It

---

[20] By the application of the vowel deletion rule (see sections 2.5.4.2), surface forms for /evdä-äm/ and /evdä-idim/ will be [evdiyäm] and [evdädim].

21 In fast speech, when the two suffixes /Imlš/ and /Idlm/ co-occur, the initial /I/ of the second suffix is deleted, as in [galajaxlmlšdlm]. Since the deletion of a vowel in fast speech is restricted to this situation (as far as I have explored), its phonology needs further explanation.

means 'be supposed to'. The latter is affixed to verbs to form perfect aspect. We can see

examples for these suffixes in the following sentences:

/lmlš/	/aj-lmlš-ldlm/ (cf. /aj/ 'hungry')	'I was supposed to be hungry.'
/mlš/	/gal-mlš-dlm/ (cf. /gal/ 'stay!')	'I had stayed.'

In Turkish, /lmlš/ and /mlš/ are called inferential and past participial, respectively (Lewis, 1967:122). Payne (1997:255) calls /mlš/ mirative in Turkish, because it conveys an unexpected and surprising information. However, in Azeri, this suffix does not have such a semantic implication, and as mentioned before it acts as a perfect aspect suffix.

There is another function of the copular suffix. It can be affixed to derived nouns[22] in the locative case to form a quasi periphrastic construction which denotes that the action specified by the verb is in progress. For example, in the sentence /yemäx-dä-yäm/ [yemäxdiyäm] 'I am in the process of eating', the derived noun /yemäx/ precedes the locative case, and the copular suffix is added to that.

The negative morpheme is no longer /mA/ in the copular construction. Instead it is

/dägil/ which is preceded by the noun, adjective, or adverb, and followed by the copular suffix, as in:

/kiši dägil-yäm/ 'I am not a man.'

1.2 The phrasal or lexical nature of nominal suffixes

It seems that suffixes like the possessive and person/number suffixes are lexically affixedto the stem, whereas the case suffix has a different behaviour, and seems to be affixed at the phrasal level. We can find support for this claim in coordinated structures where suffix suspension takes place. In a coordinate structure, when conjuncts with the same suffixes are coordinated, some or all of those suffixes must be suspended, appearing only after the second conjunct (cf. Inkelas & Orgun, 1995:765 for Turkish). Here, if a suffix must be repeated on each conjunct in a coordinate structure, it will be regarded as a lexical suffix; otherwise, it will be considered as a phrasal suffix.

We can examine this criterion for the examples in (12), meaning 'from my horses and dogs', and in (13), meaning 'my horses-ACC and my dogs-ACC':

12 (a) at -lar -Im -Inan it -lär -im -
dän horse -PL -POSS.1SG -CONJ dog
-PL -POSS.1SG -ABL

(b) * at -lar -Im -dan -Inan it -lär -im -
dän horse -PL -POSS.1SG -ABL -CONJ dog
-PL -POSS.1SG -ABL

(c) ? at -Inan it -lär -im -
dän horse -CONJ dog
-PL -POSS.1SG -ABL

13 (a) at -lar -Im -Inan it -lär -im -i
horse -PL -POSS.1SG -CONJ dog
-PL -POSS.1SG -ACC

(b) * at -lar -Im -I -Inan it -lär -im -i
horse -PL -POSS.1SG -ACC -CONJ dog
-PL -POSS.1SG -ACC

(c) ? at -Inan it -lär -im -i
horse -CONJ dog -PL -
POSS.1SG -
ACC

We can see in the above data that only the case suffixes can be suspended: in (12a) and (13a) the Ablative and Accusative suffixes are suspended whereas the other suffixes are repeated. The suspension of case suffixes is obligatory; otherwise, it will lead to ungrammatical sentences as in (12b) and (13b). If we suspend the person/number and Possessive suffixes, though the resultant sentence is grammatical as in (12c) and (13c), the first conjunct will not have the plurality and possession, i.e. resulting in a new meaning.

We can say that case suffixes are different from other nominal suffixes, and are attached postlexically; hence they are phrasal suffixes. On the other hand, suffixes like the Person/Number and Possessive suffixes are attached lexically, and hence, are lexical suffixes.

---

[22] The infinitive forms can also be used as derived nouns in Azeri.

1.3 **The distinction between derivational and inflectional verbal suffixes**

There is also a distinction among verbal suffixes based on whether they are derivational or inflectional. We will apply the same criterion, namely coordination, to distinguish among verbal suffixes. Note however that the verbal conjunction, /yIb/, unlike the nominal one, /InAn/, is derivational. One piece of evidence for considering this conjunction as derivational is that it can coordinate only verbs, whereas the nominal conjunction can also coordinate other categories like adjectives and copulas. Consider the following data:

14 (a) yey -il -yib ich -il -mä -miš -di -lär eat -PASS -CONJ drink -PASS -NEG -ASP -PAST -3PL
'They had not been eaten and drunk.'

(b) * yey -yib ich -il -mä -miš -di -lär eat -CONJ drink -PASS -NEG -ASP -PAST -3PL

(c) * yey -il -mä -miš -di -lär -yib ich -il -mä -miš -di -lär eat -PASS-NEG -ASP -PAST -PL-CONJ drink -PASS -NEG -ASP-PAST-3PL

15 (a) yey -dirt -yib ich -dirt -mä -miš -di -lär eat -CAUS -CONJ drink -

CAUS -NEG -ASP -PAST -3PL

'They had not made someone eat and drink.'

(b) * yey -yib ich -dirt -mä -miš -di -lär
eat -CONJ drink -CAUS -NEG -ASP -PAST -
3PL

(c) * yey-dirt -mä -miš -di -lär -yib ich -
dirt -mä -miš -di -lär eat-CAUS-
NEG-ASP-PAST -PL-CONJ drink-CAUS -NEG -ASP -PAST -
3PL

16 (a) yey -il -yib ich -il -mä -sä -di -lär
eat -PASS -CONJ drink -PASS -NEG -COND -
PAST -3PL
'if they were not eaten and drunk'

(b) * yey -il -mä -sä -yib ich -il -mä -sä -di -
lär eat -PASS -NEG -COND -CONJ drink -PASS -NEG -
COND -PAST -3PL

17 (a) yey -yib ich -mä -
yä -di -lär eat -CONJ
drink -NEG -SUBJ -PAST -3PL
'They probably did not eat and drink.'

(b) * yey -mä -yä -yib ich -mä -yä -di
-lär eat -NEG -SUBJ -CONJ drink -
NEG -SUBJ -PAST -3PL

As we can see in (14a) and (15a), only the passive and causative suffixes can be repeated in the second conjunct, and other suffixes, i.e. the negative, tense, and person/number suffixes are suspended. Otherwise, the ungrammatical sentences in (14b), (14c), (15b), (15c) will be derived. We can also see in (16a) and (17a) that other suffixes like the perfect aspect, and conditional mood suffixes are also suspended. Otherwise, the ungrammatical sentences in (16b) and (17b) will be derived.

Based on the above data, the Causative and Passive suffixes can not be suspended in the coordination; hence they are derivational suffixes. On the other hand, the suffixes like the Negative, Mood, Tense, Aspect, and Person/Number suffixes are obligatorily suspended, and hence they are inflectional.

1.4 Compounding

Another word-formation process in Azeri is compounding. The argument for treating compound forms as single words has a phonological and semantic basis. Phonologically, every stem has a main stress, which is usually placed on the last syllable (see section 2.7). In compound words, there is a main stress which is placed on the leftmost word. Semantically, the meaning of a compound form is not fully predictable by that of its components.

In Azeri compounding, the right-most component of a compound is its head. The following types of compounding are found in this language:

(A) N + [N]
POS
S

In this type of compounding, two nouns combine together and a possessive suffix is added to the second noun. Therefore, the two nouns come into a possessor-possessive relation to each other. We can see this process in the following examples:

/ana/	+	/dil -I/	>	/ana-dili/
'mother'		'tongue'-POSS		'mother-tongue'

/göz/	+	/yaš -I/	>	/göz-yašI/
'eye'		'wetness'-POSS		'tear'

This process is productive. Four other compounding patterns, presented below, are currently not productive.

(B) N+N

Here, two nouns combine to form a compound noun, as illustrated by the following examples:

/alIš/[23] 'buying'	+	/veriš/ 'selling'	>	/alIš-veriš/ 'trade'
/gäliš/ 'comi	+	/gediš/	>	/gäliš-gediš/

ng'	'goin g'	'relations hip'

As we see in the above examples, there is no phonological or morphological change in the words forming the compound.

(C) Adj+N

In this type of compounding, an adjective combines with a noun to form a compound word. We can see this process in the following examples:

/gIrmIzI/ 'red'	+	/badImjan/ 'egg plant'	>	/gIrmIzI-badImjan/ 'tomato'
/isti/ 'hot'	+	/ot/ 'plant'	>	/isti-ot/ 'pepper'

---

23 As we saw in section 1.2.1, the derivational suffix, /Iš/, is affixed to verbs and forms nouns as in /allš/ (cf. /al/ 'buy!').

(D) [N] + [V]
DAT
INFI

In this type of compounding, there is a combination of a noun in dative case with an infinitive verb[24]. This process forms a compound verb, as illustrated by the following examples:

/dag -ya/ + /get-mäx/ > /dagya-getmäx/
'mountain'-DAT 'go'-INFI 'to go mountaineering'

/yol -ya/ + /düš-mäx/ > /yolya-düšmäx/
'way'-DAT 'fall'-INFI 'to start'

(E) [N] + Adj
POSS

In this type of compounding, there is a combination of a noun having a possessive suffix with an adjective. This process forms compound adjectives, as shown by the following:

/dil -i/ + /širin/ > /dili-širin/
'tongue'-POSS 'sweet' 'having a speech problem'

/göz -ü/ + /ganlI/ > /gözü-ganlI/
'eye'-POSS 'bloody'

'aggressive'

1.4.1 Compounding in Persian

In this section, the same logic as for Azeri is used to identify compounds in Persian, where the main stress is placed on the left-most component of the compound. The following types of compounding are found in Persian:

(A) N + N
Possessor
Possessed

---

[24] There is one example in which there is no dative suffix, and a compound is formed with the noun innominative case:

/gulag/	+	/asmag/	>	/gulag-asmag/
'ear'		'hanging'		'listening'

This type of compounding is formed out of a possession relation between two nouns. In Persian, the possessed entity precedes the possessive marker /e/, which itself is followed by the possessor, as in:

Xane -e märiz
home -POSS sick
'The home of the sick person'

In this type of compounding, the order is reversed; that is the possessor precedes the possessed entity, and the possessive marker is also deleted, as in:

märiz -Xane
sick -home
'hospital'

However, since all of these compounds are borrowed as whole units, we regard them as borrowed words rather than Azeri compounds.

(B) N + N

A rather similar compounding process to that of Azeri (see 1.6-B) exists in Persian, wheretwo nouns form a compound, as in:

/Xärid/ 'buying'	+	/furuš/ 'selling'	>	/Xärid-furuš/ 'trade'
/räft/ 'going'	+	/amäd/ 'coming	>	/räft-amäd/ 'traffic'

We may propose that this compounding process is borrowed into Azeri to form the similar N + N compounds, although there is no independent evidence to support this claim.

The compounding processes in (C), (D), and (E) above do not occur in Persian.

1.5 Reduplication

There are three types of reduplication in this language, all of them productive. They are as follows:

1.5.1 Reduplication of nouns and adjectives

In this type, the whole noun or adjective is repeated with a change in the onset of the syllable: if the onset of the first syllable is zero, it becomes /m/; if the onset of the first syllable is not zero, it is replaced by /m/. The resultant reduplicated word denotes things related to the main noun or adjective, e.g. /agaj-magaj/= 'tree and things like that, such as plants, shrubs, etc.'. We can see this process in the following examples:

/agaj/	'tree'	/agaj-magaj/	'tree and things like that, such as flowers, etc.'
/äl/	'hand'	/äl-mäl/	'hand and things like that, such as arm, etc.'
/baš/	'head'	/baš-maš/	'head and things like that, such as neck, etc.'
/diš/	'tooth'	/diš-miš/	'tooth and things like that, such as gum, etc.'
/gara/	'black'	/gara-mara/	'black and things like this, such as stain, etc.'

As we see in the above examples, when the main word begins with a vowel, that is, the onset is zero, /m/ is added to the beginning of the reduplicated component, e.g.

/äl/>/älmäl/.

1.5.2 Reduplication of verbs

In this type, a finite verb form is repeated, and a linking morpheme is inserted between the two words. This linking morpheme is either /a/ or /ha/. An interesting point about this linking morpheme is that it does not undergo vowel harmony. The resultant reduplicated word is a noun which denotes a condition where a specific action occurs repeatedly. For example, /gälhagäl-i gördüm/ means 'I saw the repeated coming of people'. We can see this process in the following examples:

/gach/ 'run!' /gach-a-gach/

/gäl/	'come!'	/gäl-ha-gäl/
/gaz/	'dig!'	/gaz-a-gaz/
/gir/	'enter!'	/gir-ha-gir/
/tök/	'pour!'	/tök-a-tök/
/vlr/	'beat!'	/vlr-ha-vlr/

1.5.2.1 **Reduplication of verbs in the subjunctive mood**

The third person singular form of a verb in the subjunctive mood can be totally reduplicated to yield an adverb of manner. Some examples follow:

/äsyä/ 'it may blow' (subjunctive) /äsyä-äsyä/ 'in a blowing manner'

/baxya/ 'he may look' (subjunctive) /baxya-baxya/ 'while looking around or atsomething'

/gachya/ 'he may run' (subjunctive) /gachya-gachya/ 'in a running manner'

/gülyä/ 'he may laugh'(subjunctive) /gülyä-gülyä/ 'in a laughing manner'

Although the third person singular form, here, conveys a subjunctive meaning, this semantic component is not reflected in the meaning of the reduplicated adverb. Many adverbs of manner are formed in this way.

1.5.3 Reduplication of the first syllable of adjectives

The first syllable of an adjective can be repeated and the voiceless stop /p/ added as its coda, e.g. /täp-täzä/ from /täzä/. The resultant reduplicated word is an intensified adjective. Some examples are as follows:

/diri/	'alive'	/dip-diri/	'quite alive'
/gara/	'black'	/gap-gara/	'quite black'
/guru/	'dry'	/gup-guru/	'quite dry'
/täzä/	'new'	/täp-täzä/	'quite new'

This process is productive but it does not apply to those adjectives which begin with a vowel, e.g. we can not construct */ap-arlx/ from /arlx/ 'thin'.

Chapter 2

Syntax of simple clauses

Introduction

In this chapter, first we will introduce the constituent order in Azeri (section 2.2). Then, we will discuss the case system (section 2.3). The pronouns, reflexives and reciprocals are discussed in section 2.4, and in section 2.5, the passive construction in Azeri will be introduced. The copular construction will be explored in section 2.6. Then we will make a distinction between imperatives and optatives in section 2.7. In the remaining sections, the interrogative construction (section 2.8), coordination (section 2.9), and morphosyntactic borrowings in Azeri (section 2.10) will be discussed.

2.1 Constituent order

Azeri is a verb final and predominantly agglutinative language which has a case system. The surface constituent order may have no grammatical function in the language. However, this order is not completely free, and the basic order is SOV. The evidence for this order comes from the native speakers' intuitions and the examination of the Azeri texts. We can see this basic constituent order in the following example:

1 Ali kitab -I oxu -du
Ali (NOM) book -ACC read -PAST.3SG
'Ali read the book.'

There are some instances where the NP in the direct object position has no case suffix. In this instance, the constituent order is fixed and changing the order will result in pragmatically ill-formed sentences. When the direct object NP is an indefinite noun, it does not take a case. Consider the following examples:

2(a) ušag alma yey -di

child (NOM) apple eat -PAST.3SG

'The child ate (an) apple.'

(b) * alma ušag yey -di
apple (NOM) child
eat -3SG

3(a) ušag bir almayey -di
child (NOM) one apple
eat -3SG
'The child ate an apple.'

(b) * biralma ušag yey -di
one apple (NOM) childeat
-3SG

In (2a) and (3a), /ušag/ 'child' is the subject and since it is in the nominative case, there is no suffix realisation, and since the direct object in (2a) is /alma/ 'apple' which is an unspecified indefinite noun, and in (3a), it is /bir alma/ 'an apple' which is an indefinite noun, changing the order will result in sentences (2b) and (3b) which are pragmatically illformed.

Note that in Azeri, there is no definite article which can be distinguished from the demonstrative pronouns (/o/ 'that', /bu/ 'this'). The indefinite article is /bir/ 'one', as illustrated in the following example:

4 män
bir kiši gör -dü -
m I one man see -
PAST -1SG 'I saw a
man.'

When an NP does not have this indefinite article, and is marked by a case, it is definite:

5 män kiši -ni gör -dü -m
I (NOM) man -ACC see -PAST -3SG
'I saw the man.'

When there is neither an indefinite article nor a case ending, the noun is unspecified indefinite:

6 män alma yey -di -m
I (NOM) apple eat -PAST -3SG
'I ate (an) apple.'

In those sentences which have a definite object, the constituent order is free. The difference between the unmarked order and marked ones is analysable in terms of topicalisation and emphasis. Therefore, there are several possibilities for the constituent order of sentences having two arguments, i.e. subject and direct object NPs. We can see these possible constituent orders in the following examples:

7(a) Häsän kitab -I oxu -du
SOVHasan
book -ACC read -PAST.3SG
'Hasan read the book.'

(b) kitab -I Häsän oxu -du OSV

(c) kitab -I oxu -du Häsän OVS

(d) oxu -du Häsän kitab -I VSO

(e) oxu -du kitab -I Häsän VOS

However, the sentences in (7d) and (7e) seem to be odd to native speakers, though not ungrammatical. In (7b), the direct object, /kitab/ 'book' is topicalised and emphasised. In (7c) it is still topicalised but the emphasis is on the verb, /oxudu/.

When there are three arguments in the sentence, the typical order of constituents is : subject, direct object, non-direct object, and verb. Consider the following examples:

8(a) Ali kitab -I kiši -yä ver -di S DO IO
VAli (NOM) book -ACC man -DAT give -
PAST.3SG
'Ali gave the book to the man.'

(b) kitab -I Ali kiši -yä ver -di DO S IO V

(c) kitab -I kiši -yä Ali ver -di DO IO S V

(d) kiši -yä kitab -I Ali ver -di IO DO S V

(e) Ali kiši -yä kitab -I ver -di S IO DO V

(f) Ali kiši -yä ver -di kitab -I S IO V DO

(g) ver -di Ali kitab -I kiši -yä V S DO IO

As we see in (8), different constituent orders are possible for the sentence in (8a) which has the basic and unmarked order. Among these sentences, (8g), where the verb is in the initial position, seems to be odd but not ungrammatical. In sentence (8b), /kitab/ 'book' is topicalised and /kiši/ 'man' is emphasised. In (8c), /kitab/ is topicalised and *Ali* is emphasised. In (8d), /kiši/ is topicalised and *Ali* is emphasised. In (8c) and (8d), *Ali* and in (8e) and (8f), /kitab/ are extraposed.

Adverbs can also occur in free order in the clause, as illustrated below:

9(a) Ali dünän at -I bag -ya apar -dI
Ali (NOM) yesterday horse -ACC garden -DAT take -PAST.3SG

'Ali took the horse to the garden yesterday.'

(b) dünän Ali at -I bag -ya apar -dI

(c) Ali at -I dünän bag -ya apar -dI

(d) Ali dünän at -I bag -ya apar -dI

As shown in (9), the adverb /dünän/ 'yesterday' can occur in different positions within the

clause. This order also applies for the locatives, e.g. /bagda/ 'in the garden'.

Therefore, as the above data illustrates, when we change the order of constituents in an unmarked sentence, though the meaning does not change, some pragmatic differences result.

2.1.1 Basic sentence types in Azeri

There are two types of basic simple sentences in Azeri: sentences with ordinary verb forms and sentences with the copular construction. Some examples follow:

A Sentences with ordinary

verb forms 10 (a) Ali kitab -I

oxu -du

Ali book -ACC read -PAST.3SG

'Ali read the book.'

(b) Ali kitab -I oxu -ma -dI

Ali book -ACC read -NEG -PAST.3SG

'Ali did not read the book.'

B Sentences with the copular construction

11 (a) o kiši müdür -dü

that man (NOM) manager -COP.NPAST.3SG

'That man is (a) manager.'

(b) o kiši müdür -dägil

that man (NOM) manager -NEG.COP.NPAST.3SG

'That man is not (a) manager.'

14 (a) miz -in üst -ün -dä kitab var -dI
table -GEN.3SG top -POSS.3SG -LOC book EXI -COP.NPAST.3SG

'There is (a) book on the top of the table.'

(b) miz-in üst -ün -dä kitab yox -du

table -GEN.3SG top -POSS.3SG -LOC book EXI.NEG -COP.NPAST.3SG

'There is not (a) book on the top of the table.'

Within phrases, in the basic order, the modifier precedes the head; that is, adjectives and relative clauses[25] precede the noun, and adverbs or complements precede the verb, as illustrated in the following examples:

15 Ali täzä ev al -dI
Ali (NOM) new house (ACC) buy -PAST.3SG

'Ali bought (a) new house.'

16 gäl -yän kiši müdür -dü
come -REL man (NOM) manager -COP.NPAST.3SG

'The man who is coming is (a) manager.'

17 Häsän ev -yä tez gäl -di

Hasan home -DAT early come -PAST.3SG

'Hasan came home early.'

2.1.2 **Constituent order in embedded clauses**

In Azeri, some embedded clauses precede the other elements of the main clause and some others follow them. Consider the following examples:

20 biz bur -ya gäl -yän -dä Ali get -di
we here -DAT come -PRT -LOC Ali go -PAST.3SG

'When we came here, Ali went.'

21 sän alma -nI yey -yen??ä män kitab -I oxu -du -m 2SG apple -ACC eat -PRT I book -ACC read -PAST -1SG 'I read the book as soon as you ate the apple.'

22 on -un ev -dä gal -max -In -I
3SG -GEN.3SG home -LOC stay
-INFI -POSS.3SG -ACCbil -ir -di -m
know -CONT -PAST -1SG

'I knew that he stayed at home.

23 Ali bil -di ki män gäl -di -m
Ali know -PAST.3SG COMP I
come -PAST -1SG 'Ali found out that I came.'

As we see in sentences (20-22), the embedded clause precedes the other elements of the main clause, but in (23) it follows them. Embedded clauses have the same constituent order as simple sentences; that is, the verb is the final constituent of the clause.

2.2 Case system in Azeri

All nouns are inflected for case in Azeri. There are eight morphological cases, as follows: Nominative, Accusative, Dative, Ablative, Locative, Benefactive, Instrumental, and Genitive (see section 1.1.1.1). Since the genitive case should be discussed in relation with the possessive suffix, it has already been introduced in section 1.1.1.2.

2.2.1 Nominative case

The nominative case has a zero morphological realisation and thus NPs in this case are formally identical with unmarked nominals in other case relations (e.g. the indefinite noun in the accusative case). This case is required for the subject of transitive, intransitive, and copular clauses. Some examples are as follows:

24 oglan kitab -I oxu -du
boy (NOM) book -ACC read -PAST.3SG

'The boy read the book.'

25 gIz yat -dI
girl (NOM) sleep -PAST.3SG

'The girl slept.'

26 ušag aj -dI
child (NOM) hungry -COP.NPAST.3SG

'The child is hungry.'

In Azeri, since the verb agrees in person and number with its subject, it is possible to delete the subject from the clause. Consider the following examples:

27 (a) män get -di -m
I (NOM) go -PAST -1SG

'I went.'

(b) get -di -m
go -PAST -
1SG 'I went.'

2.2.2 **Accusative case**

The accusative case marks the direct object of a transitive verb, as illustrated in (24), i.e.

/kitab/ 'book'. This case surfaces as zero when the object is indefinite, as shown by the

following example:

28 Ali bir alma al -dI
Ali (NOM) one apple (ACC) buy -PAST.3SG

'Ali bought an apple.'

The non-zero realisation of the accusative case marking in Azeri is restricted to definite noun phrases.

2.2.3 Dative case

This case indicates the direction of a motion towards a person, a place, or a thing, as shown by the following examples:

29 arvad bag -ya get -di
woman (NOM) garden -DAT go -PAST.3SG

'The woman went to the garden.'

30 män kitab -I ušag -ya ver -di -m
I book -ACC child -DAT give -PAST -1SG

'I gave the book to the child.'

2.2.4 Ablative case

This case exhibits the following functions:

It specifies the place, person or thing from which the action starts:

31 oglan bag -dan gäl -di
boy (NOM) garden -ABL come -PAST.3SG

'The boy came from the garden.'

32 män alma -nI Ali -dän al -dI -m
I apple -ACCAli -ABL buy -PAST -1SG

'I bought the apple from Ali.'

II It specifies a material from which something is made:

33 kiši kif -i chärm -dän düzält-di
man (NOM) bag -ACC leather -ABL make -PAST.3SG

'The man made the bag out of leather.'

III It indicates the direction through which the action proceeds:

34 gIz häyät -dän gech -di
girl (NOM) yard -ABL pass through -PAST.3SG
'The girl passed through the yard.'

IV It can specify the cause of an action:

35 arvad chox išlä -mäx -dän naxošla -dI
woman (NOM) very work -INFI -ABL sick -PAST.3SG
'The woman became sick because of hard work.'

2.2.5 Locative case

The locative case has several functions in Azeri as follows:

I It can specify the location at which an action occurs, or the place at, in, or on which an object is located, as illustrated in the following sentences:

36 ušag mädräsä -dädärs oxu -du
child (NOM) school-LOC lesson read -PAST.3SG
'The child studied at the school.'

II In copular clauses, the noun in the locative case functions as the predicate of theclause, as shown below:

37 män ev -dä -yäm
I home -LOC -NPAST.COP.1SG

'I am at home.'

III This case also marks temporal nominals as in the following sentence:

38 Ali sahat üch -dä get -di
Ali (NOM) time three -LOC go -PAST.3SG

'Ali went at three o'clock.'

IV When this case is attached to an infinitive verb and is followed by a copularsuffix, it indicates a continuous action:

39 män yey -mäx -dä -yäm
I eat -INFI -LOC -NPAST.COP.1SG

'I am in the process of eating.'

Another function of this case is that it can attach to the verb in an embeddedclause to specify the simultaneous occurrence of two different actions, as below:

40 sän gäl -yän -dä män get -di -m
2SG (NOM) come -PRT -LOC I go -PAST -1SG
'I went when you came.'

2.2.6 **Instrumental case**

This case is used to mark an NP which is the instrument of a subject:

41 män kitab -I mIdad -Inan yaz -dI -m
I book -ACC pencil -INST write -PAST -1SG

'I wrote the book with the pencil.'

When the relevant second NP is animate, the instrumental case specifies that this NP accompanies the first one, as in the following sentence:

42 Ali Häsän -inän gäl -di
Ali (NOM) Hasan -INST come -PAST.3SG

'Ali came with Hasan.'

The /InAn/ morpheme for conjunction is different from the instrumental case suffix (see section 2.9). Consider the following example:

43 Ali -inän Häsän gäl -di -
lär Ali (NOM) -CONJ Hasan
come -PAST -3PL 'Ali and Hasan came.'

As we see in (43), the conjunction marker, unlike the instrumental case suffix is affixed to the first NP in the subject position, and the verb agrees with both NPs in this position, i.e. *Ali* and *Häsän*, while when there is an instrumental case suffix, the verb agrees only with the first NP, as shown in (42).

2.2.7 **Benefactive case**

This case is used to specify an NP which is the beneficiary of an action, as in the following example:

44 män kitab -I ušag -IchIn al -dI -m
I book -ACC child -BEN buy -PAST -1SG

'I bought the book for the child.'

2.3 Pronouns, reflexives, and reciprocals

2.3.1 Personal pronouns

The personal pronouns for the first, second and third person singular and plural in Azeri are: /män/ '1SG', /sän/ '2SG', /o/ '3SG', /biz/ '1PL', /siz/ '2PL', and /olar/ '3PL'. These pronouns are free and as for NPs, all case suffixes can be affixed to them. Thus, they can act as subject, direct object, or non-direct object in the clause, as in the following examples:

45 (a) män Ali -ni gör
-dü -m
I Ali -ACC see -PAST -1SG
'I saw Ali.'

(b) Ali män -i gör -dü
Ali (NOM) 1SG -ACC see -PAST.3SG
'Ali saw me.'

(c) Ali män -ichin gäl -di
Ali (NOM) 1SG -BEN come -PAST.3SG
'Ali came for me.'

As mentioned in section 1.1.2.1, verbs are inflected for person and number, and expectedly these agreement suffixes on the verb make it possible to delete the pronoun from the sentence. Only subjects can be deleted in this way. For example, since there is an agreement suffix, i.e. /-m/ on the verb in (45a), we can delete the pronoun, as in (46):

46 Ali -ni gör -dü -m
Ali -ACC see -PAST -
1SG 'I saw Ali.'

2.3.2 Reflexive pronoun

In Azeri, there is a reflexive pronoun /öz/ 'self' to which a possessive suffix is affixed to indicate the person and number of the NP in the nominative case. As mentioned in section 1.1.1.2, the possessive suffix is inflected for person and number.

The reflexive pronoun can act as an object in the clause by affixing a case suffix to the possessive morpheme which is already affixed to the root, as shown in the following examples:

47 (a) män öz -üm -ü ayna -da gör -dü -m
I self -POSS.1SG -ACC mirror -LOC see -PAST -
1SG

'I saw myself in the mirror.'

(b) Ali öz -ü -üchün bir kitab al -dI

Ali (NOM) self -POSS.3SG -BEN one book buy -PAST.3SG

'Ali bought a book for himself.'

In (47a), the reflexive pronoun takes the accusative case, /ü/, and acts as the direct object,and hence as a complement, while in (47b), the case suffix which is affixed to the stem is benefactive, /üchün/, and hence the reflexive is an adjunct.

When the reflexive pronoun is in the nominative case, it is emphatic, as illustrated below:

48 män öz -üm gäl -di -m

I self -POSS.1SG come -PAST -1SG

'I came myself.'

As mentioned in 2.5.1, since there is an agreement marker on the verb in Azeri, it is possible to delete the subject from the sentence. For example, the subject in (48) can be deleted, as in (49):

49 öz -üm gäl -di -m
self -POSS.1SG come -
PAST -1SG 'I came myself.'

The reflexive pronoun functions as an adjective when it precedes the head noun. In this case, it is the NP itself which takes the possessive suffix and not the reflexive. Consider the following example:

50 män öz kitab -Im -I oxu -du -m
I self book -POSS.1SG -ACC read -PAST -1SG

'I read my own book.'

There is also a reflexive suffix /un/ which is affixed to the verb and precedes all other suffixes. In this construction, the subject acts upon himself rather than upon some other person or thing, as in (51):

51 män yu -un -du -m
I wash -self -PAST
-1SG 'I washed myself.'

This suffix is no longer productive and can be affixed to few verbs, including /yu/

'wash!', /gašI/ 'scratch!', /gIz/ 'warm up!', /eš/ 'search!', /gey/ 'dress!'.

2.3.3 Reciprocal pronoun

The reciprocal pronoun is /bir bir/ 'each other' to which a possessive suffix is attached

and this suffix itself is followed by a case suffix, as illustrated in below:

52 (a) biz bir bir -imiz -ä bax -dI -x
we one one -POSS.1PL -DAT look -PAST -1PL
'We looked at each other.'

(b) siz bir bir -iz -dän ayrIl -dI -z
you one one -POSS.2PL -ABL part -PAST -2PL 'You parted from each other.'

As in the case of the reflexive pronoun, since there is an agreement marker on the verb, the subject can be deleted.

There is also a reciprocal suffix which is attached to the verb. Like the reflexive suffix, it precedes all other suffixes and is no longer productive. This suffix is /Iš/, as illustrated in the following examples:

53 (a) kiši-lär gör -üš -dü -lär
man -PL (NOM) see -RECIP -PAST -3PL

'The men met each other.'

(b) gIz -Inan oglan öp -üš -dü -lär
girl (NOM) -CONJ boy kiss -
RECIP -PAST -3PL 'The girl and the boy
kissed each other.'

As we see in (53), since the reciprocal suffix involves a mutual action, the subject must be plural as in (53a), or two NPs conjoined by a conjunction as in (53b). Note that the number marker on the verb is also plural.

The reciprocal and reflexive suffixes are mutually exclusive.

2.3.4 Demonstrative pronouns

The demonstrative pronouns in Azeri are: /bu/ 'this', /o/ 'that', /bular/ 'these', and /olar/ 'those', where it is clear that the plural pronouns are formed from the singular ones by affixing /lar/. These pronouns can take any case, and hence they can occur both as a complement or as an adjunct, as shown below:

54 bular olar -dan yaxchI -dI
-lar these(NOM) those -ABL
good -NPAST.COP -3PL 'These are
better than those.'

The singular form of demonstrative pronouns is used to specify both singular and plural head nouns, as illustrated in the following examples:

55 (a) bu ušag chox ziräk -di
this child (NOM) very clever -NPAST.COP.3SG
'This child is very clever.'

(b) bu ušag -lar chox ziräk -di -lär
this child -3PL (NOM) very clever -
NPAST.COP -3PL 'These children are very clever.'

(c) * bu -lar ušag -lar chox ziräk -di -lär
this -PL child -3PL (NOM) very clever -
NPAST.COP -3PL

As we see, (55c) is ungrammatical because the demonstrative /bu/ can not take a plural suffix. Thus, the demonstratives seem to behave like adjectives which do not take any case and number suffixes, as illustrated below:

56 (a) gara at gäl -di
black horse come -PAST.3SG
'The black horse came.'

(b) gara at -lar gäl -di -lär

black horse -PL come -PAST-3PL'The black horses came.'

(c) * gara -lar at -lar gäl -di -lär
black -PL horse -PL come -PAST -3PL

The sentence (56c) is ungrammatical because the adjective /gara/ 'black' can not take a

plural number.

In Azeri, the demonstrative pronouns for the third person are not distinguished from the third person personal pronouns, as shown in the following example:

57 o yaxchl -dl
that / 3SG (NOM) good -NPAST.COP.3SG
'That is good.' / 'He is good.'

As we see, sentence (57) is ambiguous, because the pronoun in the nominative case can be regarded either as the third person singular, or as the demonstrative pronoun for the third person singular.

There seems to be some kind of constraints on using /o/ with animate or inanimate nouns. When the subject is animate, this morpheme can be interpreted only as the third person singular morpheme. For example, since the verb, /gach/ 'run!' takes only an animate subject, the morpheme /o/ will be regarded as the personal pronoun, as in below:

58 o gach -dI
3SG(NOM) run -
PAST.3SG 'He ran.'

On the other hand, when the subject is inanimate, this morpheme will be regarded only asdemonstrative, as shown in the following example:

59 o kitab yaxchI-dI
that book (NOM) good -NPAST.COP.3SG
'That book is good.'

2.3.5 Indefinite pronouns

In Azeri, the indefinite pronouns are bimorphemic, where the first morpheme denotes indefiniteness, and the other expresses the meaning of 'person' or 'thing'. These pronouns are: /här-käs/ 'anyone', /här-šey/ 'anything', /bir-käs/ 'someone', and /bir-šey/ 'something'.

There is also an indefinite-subject pronoun, i.e. /adam/ which is used to indicate an unspecified human subject, as in below:

60 adam iš -dän yorul -ur
one (NOM) work -ABL become tired -NPAST.CONT.3SG

'One becomes tired of working.'

2.4 Passive construction

2.4.1 Introduction

This section deals with the passive construction in Azeri. We will first discuss passivisation in simple clauses, then we will examine the passive construction within complement clauses, and finally we will try to find the constraints of passivisation.

2.4.2 Passivisation in simple clauses

In Azeri, there is a passive morpheme, /Il/ which is affixed to a transitive verb to form the passive verb. The object NP which is in the accusative form becomes nominative, and is promoted to the subject position. In Azeri, the agent in the passive sentence is optional, and can be expressed preceding /väsilä-si-inän/:

61 (a) Ali mašIn -I gara? -da goy -du
Ali (NOM) car -ACC garage -LOC
put -PAST.3SG
'Ali put the car in the garage.'

(b) mašIn (Al -nin vasil -si -
car (NOM) i - ä - inän)
(Al GEN.3S mea POSS.3S -
G G

i ns INST)

gara⍰ - go -ul -
da y du

garage -LOC put -PASS -PAST.3SG

'The car was put in the garage (by Ali).'

Unlike the NP in the accusative case, NPs in other cases can not be passivised. For example, in (61a), since /mašIn/ 'car' is in the accusative case, it can be passivised, as in (61b), while in (62a), since the NP *Häsän* is in the benefactive case, it can not be passivised, as in (62 b):

62 (a) Ali Häsän -ichin bag -da gäz -di
Ali (NOM) Hasan -BEN garden -LOC search -PAST.3SG

'Ali searched for Hasan in the garden.'

(b) * Häsän bag -da (Ali -nin vasilä -si -inän) Hasan (NOM) garden -LOC (Ali -GEN.3SG means -POSS.3SG -INST)gäz -il -di

search -PASS -PAST.3SG

2.4.3 **Passive-like constructions**

In Azeri, there is a construction where an active sentence with an impersonal third personplural subject is used to express the passive meaning. Keenan (1985:247) states that this type of passives is the functional equivalent of the basic passive. Consider these examples:

63 (a) Ali ev -I düzält -di
Ali (NOM) house -ACC build -PAST.3SG
'Ali built the house.'

(b) ev düzält -il -di
house (NOM) build -PASS -PAST.3SG
'The house was built.'

(c) ev -i düzält -di -lär
house-ACC build -PAST -3PL
'They built the house. (i.e. The house was built.)'

The active sentence in (63a) can be passivised as (63b) where the direct object is promoted to the subject position and the subject is deleted. This active sentence can also be expressed as the construction in (63c) where the subject is deleted and the third person plural ending is affixed to the verb. However, there is no passive morpheme in this construction. It is more frequent than the basic passive in the spoken style of Azeri.

2.4.4 Passivisation out of complement clauses[26]

In Azeri, the subject of the complement clause can be passivised. Consider these examples:

64 (a) olar dey -ir -di -lär ki Ali märiz -di
3PL (NOM) say -CONT -PAST -3PL COMP Ali (NOM) sick -COP.NPAST.3SG

'They were saying that Ali is sick.'

(b) Ali dey -il -ir -di ki märiz -di

Ali (NOM) say -PASS -CONT -PAST.3SG COMP sick -COP.NPAST.3SG

'Ali was said to be sick.'

According to the examples in (64), passivisation is not a clause internal operation, and it can also apply across clause boundaries.

In Azeri, when the embedded verb is in the infinitive form, it is possible for both main and embedded clauses to be passivised:

65 (a) Ali alma yey -mäx -yä bašla -dI
Ali (NOM) apple eat -INFI -DAT begin -PAST.3SG

'Ali began to eat the apple.'

(b) alma -nIn yey -il -mäx -i bašla - Il -dI

apple -GEN.3SG eat -PASS -INFI -POSS begin -PASS -PAST.3SG

'Eating the apple was begun. '

In (65b), both the embedded verb /yey/ 'eat!' and the main verb /bašla/ 'begin!' take the

passive ending /Il/.

____

[26]Other analysis of this passivisation might be considered, but they still seem to relay on the grammaticality of this sentence:

* Ali dey -il -ir -di
Ali (NOM) say -PASS -CONT -PAST.3SG
ki o märiz -di
COMP 3SG sick -COP.NPAST.3SG

2.4.5 Constraints on the passive construction

The following constraints apply to the passive construction in Azeri.

I Case constraint: In Azeri, only the NP in the accusative case can be promoted to the subject position in passivisation. The sentences in (66) illustrate this constraint:

66 (a) Ali kitab -I bag -da Häsän -yä ver -di
Ali (NOM) book -ACC garden -LOCHasan -DAT give -PAST.3SG

'Ali gave the book to Hasan in the garden.'

(b) kitab bag -da Häsän -yä ver -il -di
book (NOM) garden -LOC Hasan -DAT give -PASS -PAST.3SG

'The book was given to Hasan in the garden.'

(c) * bag kitab -I Häsän -yä ver -il -di
garden (NOM) book -ACC Hasan -DAT give -PASS -PAST.3SG

(d) * Häsän kitab -I bag -da ver -il -di
Hasan (NOM) book -ACC garden -LOC give -PASS -PAST.3SG

II Causativity constraint: In Azeri, passivisation is blocked by causativity. That is, when the verb is in the causative form, it can not be passivised. The examples in (67) illustrate this constraint:

67 (a) Häsän alma -nI yey -di
Hasan (NOM) apple -ACC eat -PAST.3SG

'Hasan ate the apple.'

(b) alma yey -il -di
apple (NOM) eat -PASS -PAST.3SG

'The apple was eaten.'

(c) Ali alma -nI Häsän -yä yey -dirt -di
Ali (NOM) apple -ACC Hasan -DAT eat -CAUS -PAST.3SG

'Ali made Hasan eat the apple.'

(d) * alma Häsän -yä yey -dirt -il -di
apple (NOM) Hasan -DAT eat -CAUS -PASS -PAST.3SG

2.5 Copular construction

The copular clause is used to express properties, temporal and locational presence and possession. Consider these examples:

72 (män) aj -yam[27]
I (NOM) hungry (NOM) -COP.NPAST.1SG

'I am hungry.'

In (72), the clause has an argument /män/ 'I', which is the subject, and a predicate, /aj/ 'hungry'. If /män/ 'I' is deleted, the sentence is still grammatical because of the agreement marker on the copula. Note that the copula is inflected for tense and person/number. These inflections are different from that of verbs (see section 1.1.3). To occur with aspect or mood suffixes, the copular suffix is preceded by the verb /ol/ 'become' which is followed by the aspect or mood suffixes, as in (73):

73 män aj ol -muš[28] -yam
I (NOM) hungry (NOM) become -ASP -COP.NPAST.1SG

'I have become hungry.'

In the copular clause, two NPs can occur in the nominative case, where the second NP predicates different attributes of the first one.

As mentioned in section 1.1.3, the negative morpheme for the copular construction is different from that of verbal predicates, as shown below:

74 (a) män bag -dan gäl -mä -di -m
I garden -ABL come -NEG -PAST -1SG
'I did not come from the garden.'

(b) män bag -da dägil -yäm
I garden -LOC NEG -COP.NPAST.1SG
'I am not in the garden.'

---

[27] In Lee's (1996) study, the copular suffix has been mentioned with an initial glide within parenthesis, i.e. *(y)am*, and the underlying form is not discussed.

As we see in (74a), the negative morpheme /mä/ is affixed to the verb and is followed by other suffixes. In (74b), the negative morpheme is /dägil/, which precedes the copula. This negative morpheme seems to be free because unlike other suffixes, its vowels are not necessarily in harmony with that of the preceding morpheme.

When an indefinite noun is used as the predicate in the copular clause, it does not need the indefinite marker, /bir/ 'one', as illustrated in (75):

75 Ali šagird -di
Ali (NOM) student (NOM) -COP.NPAST.3SG
'Ali is a student.'

If the indefinite marker precedes the noun, it emphasises that noun. For example, if we say the sentence in (75) as:

76 Ali bir šagird -di
Ali (NOM) one student (NOM) -COP.NPAST.3SG
'Ali is a student.'

it means that Ali is *a student* and not, e.g. *a teacher*.

To form a copular clause in the future, the verb /ol/ 'become' is followed by the copular

suffix, as shown in below:

77 män bag -da xästä ol -yajax -yam
I garden -LOC tired become -FUT -COP.NPAST.1SG
'I will be tired in the garden.'

The copula is also used to construct existential clauses, periphrastic tense constructions, and cleft constructions. These will be discussed in the following sections.

2.5.1 Existential constructions

To construct existential clauses, the copular suffix is preceded by the existential morpheme, /var/, as in below:

78 bir agaj bag -da var -dI
one tree (NOM) garden -LOC EXI -COP.NPAST.3SG
'There is a tree in the garden.'

The negative alternative for /var/ is the morpheme /yox/ 'no', as in (79):

79 bir agaj bag -da yox -du
one tree (NOM) garden -LOC EXI.NEG -
COP.NPAST.3SG

'There is not a tree in the garden.'

The copular construction containing /var/ can also be used to express possession where a possessive suffix is affixed to /var/, while in the non-existential clauses, it is affixed to the possessed entity. Consider the following examples:

80 (a) män -im kitab -Im täzä -di
I - book POSS.1S new -
GEN.1SG G COP.NPAST.3SG
'My book is new.'

(b) män -im kitab var -Im -dI

I -GEN.1SG book EXI -POSS.1SG -COP.NPAST.3SG
'I have a book.'

In (80b), the possessive suffix /Im/ is affixed to /var/, unlike in (80a) where this suffix is

attached to the possessed entity, i.e. /kitab/ 'book'.

In existential clauses as in verbal clauses, the word order is relatively free. Consider these examples:

81 (a) bir guš bag -da var -dI
one sparrow (NOM) garden -LOC EXI -
COP.NPAST.3SG
'There is a sparrow in the garden.'

(b) bag -da bir guš var -dI
garden -LOC one sparrow (NOM) EXI -
COP.NPAST.3SG
'There is a sparrow in the garden.'

The order in (81a) is the most frequent (unmarked order), which seems to go against the generalisation suggested by Clark (1978:88). She claims that indefinite nominals like *a book* do not occur in initial position of existential clauses and this reflects a general discourse constraint: given information is given by definite nominals and introduced before new information which is signalled by indefinite nominals.

2.5.2 Periphrastic constructions

The copula in Azeri is used to form periphrastic tense constructions. The first one is formed by affixing the locative case suffix to an infinitive verb which is followed by the copula, and denotes an action which is in progress. Consider the following example:

82 män yey -mäx -dä -yäm
I eat -INFI -LOC -COP.NPAST.1SG
'I am in the process of eating.'

There is another periphrastic construction, where the copula is used to form a future tense. In this construction, the verb which has already the derivational suffix /yAjAx/ is followed by the copula, as in the following example:

83 män yey -yäjäx -yäm
I eat -FUT -COP.NPAST.1SG
'I will eat.'

2.5.3 Cleft clause constructions

The copula in Azeri can be used to present the subject as the focus in a cleft clause. Heine and Reh (1984:109-110) have shown that in a cleft structure like NP + copula + subordinate clause, the new information which is expressed by the sentence-initial constituent is foregrounded and the presupposed information is encoded in the subordinate clause. This is true in Azeri, where the copula is used to form a cleft clause, focusing the subject, as shown below:

84 (a) män get -ir -äm
I go -CONT -NPAST.1SG
'I am going.'

(b) män -yäm ki get -ir -äm
I -COP.NPAST.1SG COMP go -CONT -NPAST.1SG
'It is me who is going.'

(c) o get -yän män -yäm
that go REL I -COP.NPAST.1SG
'It is me who is going.'

As shown in (84b-c), the subject /män/ 'I' is the focus of the sentence, and as Heine and

Reh (1984:147, 182) say, the copula is desemantisized to a focus marker.

2.6 Imperatives and optatives

It seems that there are two true imperatives in Azeri: the second person singular and the second person plural. The former surfaces as zero and the latter as /Iz/ (see section 1.1.2.5). There are some other suffixes for the first and third person which look like imperatives, as they are treated in Turkish by Lewis (1967). However, the behaviour of these suffixes is different from true imperatives at least in Azeri, and they are considered here as optatives (see section 1.1.2.5). In the following section, we will introduce these true imperatives, and then will discuss how they differ from optatives.

The imperative suffix occurs following valency changing suffixes (i.e. passive and causative) and the negative suffix, /mA/. No other suffixes can occur with imperative suffixes, as illustrated below:

85 Ali -ni otur -t -ma
Ali -ACC sit -CAUS -NEG (IMP.2SG)
'Do not make Ali sit.'

There are certain structural restrictions for the first and third person suffixes which do notapply to the second person. These restrictions illustrate that the behaviour of the former is different from the latter which is a true imperative. Based on the following observations, we can call the first and third person suffixes optative rather than imperative.

2.6.1 Differences between 1st and 3rd person suffixes and 2nd person suffixes

Davies (1986:99) suggests two properties for imperatives which distinguish them from other types of clauses. The first property is that an imperative does not inflect for tense, and the second is that it never allows a modal. If we use these properties to distinguish among imperatives and optatives in Azeri, we can find a distinction between them. Although neither of them takes a tense, the first and third person suffixes can take a modal like /šayäd/ 'may', while the second person can not, as illustrated below:

86 (a) biz (šayäd) bag -ya get -yäx
1PL (NOM) may garden -DAT go -OPT.1PL
'We (may) go to the garden.'

(b) * siz (šayäd) bag -ya get -yiz
2PL (NOM) may garden -DAT go -IMP.2PL

(c) olar (šayäd bag -ya get -sin -lär

3PL (NOM) may garden -DAT go -OPT -3PL

'They (may) go to the garden.'

Thus, we may say that the morphosyntactic function of the second person suffixes is different from that of others.

Furthermore, the verb for the first and third person suffixes conveys the speaker's desire

or suggestion which may be adhered to. Consider the following examples:

87 (a) män bag -ya get -yim

I garden -DAT go -OPT.1SG

'I (might) go to the garden. (i.e. It is better for me to go to the garden.)'

(b) o bag -ya get -sin

3SG (NOM) garden -DAT go -OPT.2SG

'He (might) go to the garden. (i.e. It is better for him to go to the garden.)'

In (87a), the speaker expresses a desire for going to the garden, and in (87b), he makes a suggestion for a third person to go to the garden, which may be followed.

On the other hand, for the second person, the verb conveys an order rather than a desire or suggestion, as shown below:

88 (a) sän bag -ya get
2SG (NOM) garden - DAT go (IMP.2SG)
'(You) go to the garden.'

(b) siz ävväl nahar yey -yiz
2PL (NOM) first lunch eat -IMP (2PL)
'(You PL) first eat lunch.'

There is another difference between these suffixes. The first and third person suffixes canform a yes-no question by putting a rising intonation on the suffix, but the second person can not, as in:

89 (a) get -yim
?go - OPT.1SG
'(May) I go? (i.e. Do you want me to go?)'

(b) * get ?
go (IMP.2SG)

(c) get -sin
?go -OPT.3SG
'(May) he go? (i.e. Do you want him to go?)'

The distinction between true imperatives and other suffixes is also discussed in the literature extensively. Lyons (1977:747) claims that the imperative can only be second person and not even third person. Palmer (1986:111) in discussing first and third person forms as imperatives suggests that:

> "The essential question is whether all or any of these 1st and 3rd person forms are 'true' imperatives. If the Imperative is defined as presenting a proposition for action by the hearer, then clearly it can only be 2nd person. But could it not be presented for action by someone else, even though it is the hearer who is addressed?"

He concludes that there is no definite answer to this question and hence suggests that it may be best if we restrict the term 'imperative' to second person forms and to use the term 'Jussive' for other forms.

Sadock and Zwicky (1985:177), studying 23 languages state that the imperative form for the first or third person expresses a desire and this form is called Hortative which is formally distinct from the imperative.

Based on the above-mentioned distinctions between the first and third person suffixes on the one hand and the second person suffixes on the other hand, we can suggest that the former are optative suffixes, while the latter are true imperative suffixes in Azeri[29].

2.6.2 Constraints on imperatives in Azeri

There are various claims about syntactic-semantic constraints on the distribution of certain categories with imperatives. Davies (1986:11-18) discusses these claims and rules them out by providing counter-examples in English. Some of these claims seem to be supported by Azeri examples and for some others, we can find counter-examples in this language. In the following section, we will examine Azeri data against these claims.

Davies (1986:14) discusses the claim that some predicates can be acceptable in a negative imperative but not in a positive one, as in :

90 (a) Do not feel disappointed.
(b) ? Feel disappointed.

In Azeri, unlike English, there is no difference between the negative and positive forms of such imperatives in terms of acceptability, as illustrated below:

91 (a) mäyus ol -mä[30]

[29] Lee (1996) has regarded all these suffixes as imperatives. However, when he mentions them in embedded clauses, he uses the term 'subjunctive' to refer to the first and third person suffixes.

disappointed be -NEG (IMP.2SG)

'Do not be disappointed.'

(b) mäyus ol
disappointed
be
(IMP.2SG)

'Be disappointed. (e.g. when someone suggests that a friend should give uplooking for something.)'

Another claim is about a syntactic constraint which does not allow certain verbs to be made imperative (e.g see Stockwell et al. 1973:651; Brown and Miller, 1980:326-237). It is claimed that for example the following sentences are odd in English:

92 (a) ? Understand the answer.
(b) ? Want more money.
(c) ? Hope it rains.

Brown and Miller suggest that the propositional structure of imperatives must have an action verb and an agent participant. Davies (1986:13) objects to this claim and gives some examples where the verb is stative rather than an action verb, but the imperative sentence is still grammatical:

93 (a) Know the poem by Friday.
(b) Stop moaning and hope for the best.

In Azeri, there is also no such constraint on the occurrence of stative verbs as imperatives, as we can see in these examples:

94 (a) javab -I anla
answer -ACC understand (IMP.2SG)
'Understand the answer. (e.g. when a teacher suggests that a student should understand the answer before telling it).'

(b) chox pul istä
more money (ACC) want (IMP.2SG)
'Want more money. (e.g. when a girl encourages her older brother to get more pocket money from the father).'

(c) ümidivar ol ki yaglš yag -ya

---

[30] Lee (1996) considers the negative imperative forms as 'prohibitive' which is formed by adding the negative suffix to the stem.

hopefulbe (IMP.2SG) COMP rain rain - SUBJ.3SG

'Hope it rains. (e.g. when someone encourages a farmer to be hopeful for the rain).'

Thorne (1966:70-71) states that there are certain kinds of imperatives where it is not obvious whether the subject is an underlying *you* as in :

95 (a) Nobody move.
(b) Everybody get out as quick as he/you can.
(c) Somebody pay the bill.
(d) John pay the bill.
(e) Sit down, boys.

He, unlike others, does not consider the subject in (95a-c) as the third person, but as vocative. Thus, he suggests that nouns as the subject of imperatives require the feature

[+ vocative], and this feature is always realised by *you* either as a determiner on the noun, as in *you boys come here*, or by *you* itself.

However, Stockwell et al. (1973:640-641) object to Thorne by distinguishing between the sentences in (95a-c) and in (95e-d) based on intonation. They claim that the latter require a comma-intonation to be considered vocative. Furthermore, in sentences like (95d), it isnot possible to refer to *John* by a third person pronoun, as in:

96 (a) John, take off
your coat.
(b) * John
take off his
coat.

On the other hand, the sentences in (95a-c) do not require comma-intonation after the subject and admit the third person pronominal reference:

97 (a) Somebody, take off your coat.
(b) Somebody take off his coat.

In Azeri, a formal distinction can be made between the use of the vocative and that of thethird person suffix (i. e. optatives). Consider the following examples

98 (a) Ali gäl ev -yä
Ali (NOM) come
(IMP.2SG) home-
DAT'Ali, come home.'

(b) Ali gäl -sin ev -yä
Ali (NOM) come -OPT.3SG home -DAT'Ali (may) come home.'

99 (a) bir näfär kot -un -u chIxart
one person coat -POSS.2SG -ACC take off (IMP.2SG)

'Somebody, take off your coat.'

(b) bir näfär kot -un -u chIxart -sIn

one person coat -POSS.3SG -ACC take off -OPT.3SG

'Somebody (may) take off his coat.'

In (98a), *Ali* is a vocative and the verb is in the imperative form for the second person, while in (98b), it is the third person subject and the verb contains the third person optative suffix. Similarly, in (99a), /bir näfär/ 'somebody' is a vocative and the verb has a secondperson imperative ending, while in (99b), it is the subject, and the verb contains a third person optative ending. Thus, the vocative NP occurs with the second person imperative and the third person subject NP occurs with the third person optative.

Besides this formal distinction, there is also an intonational difference between vocatives and third person subjects in Azeri. Following the vocative, there is a pause, while there isno such a pause after the third person subject.

Katz and Postal (1964:75) claim that *yourself* is the only reflexive pronoun that can occurin imperative sentences: *wash yourself*, not *wash himself*. However, in Azeri, it is also possible for *himself* to occur in an imperative sentence. For example, when a mother asksher daughter to wash her brother but not his clothes, she says:

100 öz -ü -nü yu[31]
self -POSS.3SG -ACC wash (IMP.2SG)
'Wash himself.'

2.7 Interrogative construction

In this section, we will discuss two types of question formation process: yes-no questions, and wh-questions.

2.7.1 Yes-no questions

In Azeri, yes-no questions are only formed by putting a rising intonation on the final word, as illustrated below:

101 (a) o dünän gäl -di
3SG (NOM) yesterday come -PAST.3SG

'He came yesterday.'

(b) o dünän gäl -di
?3SG (NOM) yesterday
come -
PAST.3SG 'Did he come
yesterday?'

As we see in (101), there is no Movement and no question morpheme in yes-no question formation of Azeri, and only the intonation of the sentence is changed.

2.7.2 WH-questions

In Azeri, a wh-question is formed by inserting an appropriate wh constituent instead of the constituent which is being questioned. There are three wh constituents in Azeri:

/hara/ 'where', /näy/ 'what', /kim/ 'who'. They are inflected for case, and form some

other wh constituents. Some examples follow:

102 (a) Ali kitab -I Häsän -yä ver -di
Ali (NOM) book -ACC Hasan -DAT give -PAST.3SG
'Ali gave the book to Hasan.'

(b) Ali näy -i Häsän -yä ver -di
?Ali (NOM) what -ACC
Hasan -DAT give -PAST.3SG 'What did Ali give to Hasan?'

(c) Ali kitab -I kim -yä ver -di
?Ali (NOM) book -ACC who -DAT
give -PAST.3SG 'To whom did Ali give the book?'

Based on the above sentences, we can say that in wh question formation in Azeri, the wh constituent appears in the base-generated position at S-structure, that is, there is no overt WH Movement for such a construction in this language.

Another piece of evidence for the above claim comes from the formation of the indirect question, as in below:

103 o män -dän soruš -du ki
3SG (NOM) I -ABL ask -PAST.3SG COMP
kim -inän danIš -dI -m
who -INST speak -PAST
-1SG 'He asked me who I talked to.'

As we see, to form the indirect question in Azeri , the wh constituent is inserted instead ofthe constituent which is being questioned, and a complementiser is inserted preceding thewh clause and subject-verb agreement takes place.

However, in marked constituent order it is possible to shift wh constituent to the initial position of the sentence as in topicalisation. The examples in (104) show such promotion:

104 (a) o näy -i sän -yä ver -di
?3SG (NOM) what -ACC
2SG -DAT give -PAST.3SG
'What did he give to you?'

(b) näy -i o sän -yä ver -di
?what -ACC 3SG (NOM) 2SG -DAT
give -PAST.3SG 'What did he give to you?'

2.8 Coordination

In Azeri, coordinate structures exhibit universal properties of coordination, e.g. only constituents belonging to the same category can be conjoined. However, there are different conjunction markers for NPs and VPs. Here, we discuss the coordination of both categories, in turn.

2.8.1 NP coordination

There are two conjunction morphemes for NPs. The native conjunction marker is the suffix /-InAn/, which is affixed to the first coordinated constituent, while the borrowed Persian conjunction marker, /vä/, is a separate word. Consider the following examples:

105 (a) kiši -inän oglan get -di -lär
man -CONJ boy go
-PAST -3PL 'The man and the
boy went.'

(b) kiši vä oglan get -di -lär
man CONJ boy go
-PAST -3PL 'The man and the
boy went.'

As we see in (105a-b), the conjunction markers /-InAn/ and /vä/ follow the first NP, /kiši/ 'man', and the verb agrees with the whole conjoined noun phrase. The conjunction marker /-InAn/ has a different function from the homophonous instrumental case suffix,

/-InAn/, which is affixed to the second NP (see section 2.1.6), as in :

106 o kiši oglan -Inan get -di
that man boy -INST go -PAST -3SG

'The man went with the boy.'

In this sentence, the verb agrees only with /ki�i/ 'man' which is the subject, while in

(105a), the verb is plural since it agrees in number with the whole conjoined noun phrase,

i.e. /ki�i/ CONJ /oglan/.

Up to this point, we assumed that the conjunction /vä/ is a separate word and not a suffix. A piece of evidence for this claim comes from word stress. This conjunction can be stressed in certain contexts. For example when the speaker says:

107 Ali vä Häsän get -di -lär
Ali CONJ Hasan go -PAST - 3PL
'Ali and Hasan went.'

and the hearer asks: "I did not hear you. Did Ali go alone?" the speaker repeats the sentence in (107) by putting stress on the conjunction /vä/. The conjunction /-InAn/, unlike /vä/, can not be stressed.

Another piece of evidence is that we can put a pause before the conjunction /vä/ like any other word, while the pause is not possible for a suffix like the conjunction /-InAn/.

When coordinate NPs are inanimate, the agreement on the verb is singular, as illustrated in below[32]:

108 (a) uzun yol -Inan agur yük on -u yor - du

long road -CONJ heavy load 3SG -ACC exhaust -PAST.3SG

'The long road and heavy load exhausted him.'

(b) * uzun yol -Inan agur yük on -u yor -du -lar long road -CONJ heavy load 3SG -ACC exhaust -PAST -3PL

In the coordination within existential clauses, the copula is always singular, as shown in this example:

109 burda bir kiši -inän bir oglan var -dI
here one man -CONJ one boy EXI -COP.NPAST.3SG

'There are a man and a boy here.'

It is also possible for the inanimate coordinate NPs to occur without a conjunction marker. In this case, there is a pause after the first NP. For example, the sentence in

(108) can be stated as follows:

110 uzun yol agur yük on -u yor -du
long road heavy load 3SG -ACC exhaust -PAST.3SG

'The long way and heavy load exhausted him.'

[32] Since there is no syntactic difference in the coordinate constructions using /-InAn/ or /vä/, we illustrate examples only with the first one.

The deletion of the conjunction marker is not possible for the animate NPs in (105) as illustrated in below:

111 * kiši oglan get -di -lär
man boy go -PAST -
3PL

There are certain coordinate NPs which are semantically related, and where it is possible to delete the conjunction marker from the sentence, as illustrated in these examples:

112 (a) är arvad get -di -lär
husband
wife go -PAST -
3PL 'The husband and the
wife went.'

(b) goyun gechi ot -I yey -di -lär
sheep goat grass -ACC eat- -3PL
PAST
'The sheep and the goat ate grass.'

(c) at bu -dan gech -di -lär
gat r
Ir
horse he -ABL pass -PAST -
mule re through 3PL
'The horse and the mule passed through here.'

(d) Ali bag -ya daš gum gätir -di

Ali (NOM) garden -DAT stone pebble bring -
PAST.3SG

'Ali brought stone and pebble to the garden.'

Since /är/ 'husband' and /arvad/ 'wife' in (112a), /goyun/ 'sheep' and /gechi/ 'goat' in (112b), /at/ 'horse' and /gatIr/ 'mule' in (112c), and /daš/ 'stone' and /gum/ 'pebble' in (112d) are semantically related, it is possible to delete the conjunction marker.

However, the order for these coordinate NPs is fixed. Thus, the first NP always occurs first, otherwise the sentence will be ungrammatical. For example, if we change the order of NPs in (112a), the sentence will be ungrammatical:

113 * arvad	är	get -di -lär
wife	husband	go -PAST -3PL

Therefore, it seems that this type of coordinate NPs is in fact idiomatic. That is, it is a conjunction in the lexical level, unlike other syntactic conjunctions.

One piece of evidence to support this claim is that we can not coordinate any semantically related NPs as we can these NPs. Consider this example:

114 * päšä milchäk uch -du -
larfly mosquito fly
-PAST -3PL

In (114), although the two NPs /päšä/ 'fly' and /milchäk/ 'mosquito' are semantically

related, they can not be coordinated without the conjunction.

When there are more than two coordinate NPs, all of them except the last one take the conjunction marker, as in the following example:

115 män kitab -Inan miz -inän sändäli -ni gätir -di -m
I book -CONJ table -CONJ chair -ACC bring -
PAST -1SG

'I brought the book, the table, and the chair.'

In NP coordination, the case suffixes are suspended from the first NP, as illustrated below:

116 gara kitab -Inan ag miz -i gätir -di -m
black book -CONJ white table -ACC bring -
PAST -1SG 'I brought the black book and the
white table.'

In (116), the accusative case suffix, /i/, is suspended from the first NP, /gara kitab/ 'the black book'. However, if we suspend the possessive suffix, the sentence will be ambiguous. Consider the following examples:

117 (a) at -lar -Im -Inan it -lär -im -i gätir -di -m
horse -PL -POSS.1SG -CONJ dog -PL -POSS.1SG -ACC
bring -PAST -1SG
'I brought my horses and my dogs.'

(b) at -lar -Inan it -lär -im -i gätir -di -m
horse -PL -CONJ dog -PL -POSS.1SG
-ACC bring -PAST -1SG 'I brought the
horses and my dogs.'

or 'I brought my horses and my dogs.'

As we see in (117b), when the possessive suffix is suspended, either both NPs or only the second NP can be regarded as the possessed entity.

2.8.2 **VP coordination**

There are three possibilities for VP coordination. First, verb phrases can be coordinated by a conjunction marker which is different from that of NPs. This conjunction marker is /ylb/ which is affixed to the first verb, and all other suffixes except valency-changing ones are suspended from the first verb, as illustrated below:

118 (a) kiši kitab -I götür -yüb get -di

man book -ACC pick up -CONJ go -PAST.3SG

'The man picked up the book and went.'

(b) kiši kitab -I götür -yüb ušag -ya ver -di

man book -ACC pick up -CONJ child -DAT give -PAST.3SG

'The man picked up the book and gave it to the child.'

As we see in (118a), the conjunction marker, /yib/ is affixed to the first verb stem, /götür/

'pick up!', and the past tense and third person plural suffixes are suspended.

Another possibility for VP coordination is to use the borrowed conjunction marker, /vä/

'and':

119 (a) kiši kitab -I götür -dü vä get -di
man book -ACC pick up -PAST.3SG CONJ go -PAST.3SG

'The man picked up the book and went.'

(b) kiši kitab -I götür -dü vä ušag -ya ver -di

man book -ACC pick up -PAST.3SG CONJ child -DAT give -PAST.3SG

'The man picked up the book and gave it to the child.'

In the third type of verb coordination, there is a pause after each verb, without using a conjunction marker. In this form, too, no suffix is suspended, as shown below:

120 (a) kiši kitab -I götür -dü get -di
man book -ACC pick up -PAST.3SG go -PAST.3SG
'The man picked up the book and went.'

(b) kiši kitab -I götür -dü ušag -ya ver -di

man book -ACC pick up -PAST.3SG child -DAT give -PAST.3SG

'The man picked up the book and gave it to the child.'

2.8.3 **Other conjunctions**

There are other conjunction markers which are borrowed from Persian. They coordinate two NPs or two VPs by denoting inclusion or exclusion. These conjunction markers are :

/ya/ 'or', /ya....ya/ 'either...or', /häm....häm/ 'both....and', /nä.....nä/ 'neither...nor'. Some

examples follow:

121 (a) kiši ya oglan get -di
man CONJ boy go -PAST.-3SG

'The man or the boy went.'

(b) kiši gäl -di ya get -di
man come -PAST.3SG CONJ go -PAST.-3SG
'The man came or went.'

122 (a) ya kiši ya oglan get -di
CONJ man CONJ boy go -PAST.-3SG
'Either the man or the boy went.'

(b) kiši ya get -di ya gäl -di

man CONJgo -PAST.3SG CONJ come -PAST.3SG

'The man either went or came.'

123 (a) nä kiši nä oglan get -di
CONJ man CONJ boy go -PAST.3SG

'Neither the man nor the boy went.'

(b) kiši nä get -di nä gäl -di
man CONJgo -PAST.3SG CONJ come -PAST.3SG

'The man neither went nor came.'

124 (a) häm kiši häm oglan get -di-lär CONJ man CONJ boy go -PAST -3PL 'Both the man and the boy went.'

(b) kiši häm get -di häm gäl -di

man CONJgo -PAST.3SG CONJ come -PAST.3SG

'The man both went and came.'

In (121-123), the number of the verb is always singular, since these conjunction markers unlike /-InAn/, and /vä/, illustrate exclusion, while in (124a), the number is plural, because it denotes inclusion. All of these conjunction markers are recursive and can coordinate several phrases, as illustrated in these examples:

125 (a) häm kiši häm oglan häm arvad get -di -lär
CONJ man CONJ boy CONJ woman go -PAST -3PL 'The man and the boy and the woman went.'

(b) kiši häm get -di häm gäl -di häm yat -dI
man CONJ go -PAST.3SG CONJ come-PAST.3SG CONJ sleep -PAST.3SG
'The man went and came and slept.

In (124), the English gloss 'both' is used to convey a closer glossing of this type of conjunction in Azeri where the same conjunction /häm/ is repeated. Payne (1985:22), discussing these conjunction markers in Persian, uses the same gloss.

Chapter 3
Syntax of complex clauses

Introduction

In this chapter, first causative constructions in Azeri will be discussed. In section 3.3, embedded clauses including complement and adjunct clauses will be explored. Two types of adjunct clauses will be discussed in section 3.1.2: adverbial clauses and relative clauses.

3.1 Causative constructions

3.1.1 Introduction

This section deals with causative constructions in Azeri. We will introduce both morphological and syntactic causativisation strategies in this language along with their constraints. We will also examine the data against the accessibility hierarchy theory (Comrie, 1989). Then, in the rest of the section, double causativity, causativisation of compound verbs, and the interaction of causativisation and passivisation will be explored.

3.1.2 Morphological causatives

In Azeri, there is a causative morpheme, /dlr/[33], which is productive, and can be affixed to any verb stem to form a causative verb. Some examples of causative verbs in Azeri are illustrated below:

/ach-dl/	'he opened'	/ach-dlr-dl/	'he made someone open'
/gül-dü/	'he laughed'	/gül-dür-dü/	'he made someone laugh'
/yaz-dl/	'he wrote'	/yaz-dlr-dl/	'he made someone write'

---

[33] In this morpheme, the vowel is affected by vowel harmony, while the /dIr ~ Irt ~ t/ alternation is conditioned by other factors. For details on the allomorphic distribution of this suffix see section 1.1.2.7.

To form a causative sentence in Azeri, the causer takes the subject position, and the causee occurs as the direct or non-direct object, as illustrated by the following sentence:

1 män Ali -ni dur -dur -du -m
I Ali -ACC stand -CAUS -PAST -1SG
'I made Ali stand up.'

Causatives of transitive verbs involve two objects:

2 (a) Häsän kitab -I oxu -du
Hasan(NOM) book -ACC read -PAST.3SG 'Hasan read the book.'

(b) Ali kitab -I Häsän -yä oxu -t -du
Ali(NOM) book -ACC Hasan -DAT read -CAUS -PAST.3SG 'Ali made Hasan read the book.'

As we see, the direct object of the causativised verb, i.e. /kitab/ is the same as in the non- causative clause, and the causee, i.e. *Häsän* becomes the non-direct object in the causative clause.

When the object of the non-causative clause is non-direct, it remains non-direct in the causative clause, and the causee becomes the direct object, as the following examples illustrate:

3 (a)	Häsän	at	-ya	min[34]	-di
	Hasan(NOM)	horse	-DAT	get on	-PAST.3SG

'Hasan got on the horse.'

(b) Ali Häsän -i at -ya min -dir -di
Ali(NOM) Hasan -ACC horse -DAT get on -CAUS -PAST.3SG 'Ali made Hasan get on the horse.'

In other words, when the direct object position is already occupied, the causee takes the non-direct object position as in (2); if the direct object position is not occupied, the causee takes the direct object position as in (3).

---

[34] /min/ 'get on!' belongs to the class II of verb classes (see section 2.4.3).

3.1.3 Syntactic causatives

This causativisation strategy has been borrowed from Persian, and is used both by those who have had at least a primary education and those who have not. Consider the following sentences:

4 (a) Ali yat -dI
Ali (NOM) sleep -PAST.3SG
'Ali slept.'

(b) män bayls ol -du -m (ki) Ali yat -ya
I (NOM) cause -PAST -1SG (COMP) Ali (NOM) sleep -SUBJ.3SG
'I caused Ali to sleep.'

5 (a) män yat -dI -m
I sleep -PAST -1SG
'I slept.'

(b) o bayls ol -du (ki) män yat -ya -m
3SG (NOM) cause -PAST.3SG (COMP) I sleep -SUBJ -1SG 'He caused me to sleep.'

The causative sentences in (4b) and (5b) occur as embedded clauses preceded by the compound verb /bayls ol/ 'cause!'. The word /bayls/ 'cause' can also occur separately as a noun.

3.1.4 Case assignment and the case hierarchy

The case assigned to NPs in causative clauses can be predicted using Comrie's case hierarchy, where he claims that the hierarchy of grammatical categories is as follows: subject > direct object > indirect object > oblique object. According to Comrie, the causee occupies the leftmost position on this hierarchy that is not already filled (Comrie, 1989:176).

3.1.5 Constraints on causativisation

3.1.5.1 A constraint on the causativisation of ditransitive clauses

There is a constraint on the causativisation of ditransitive clauses (i.e. clauses having a direct object and one or more non-direct objects) in Azeri: when these clauses are morphologically causativised, the causee must be deleted; otherwise, the output will be ungrammatical, as shown by the following sentences:

6 (a) Häsän kitab -I Ali -yä ver -di
Hasan(NOM) book -ACC Ali -DAT
give -PAST.3SG 'Hasan gave the
book to Ali.'

(b) män kitab -I Ali -yä ver -dir -di -m
I book -ACC Ali -DAT give -CAUS -PAST -1SG
'I made (someone) give the book to Ali.'

(c) * män kitab -I Häsän -yä Ali -yä ver -dir -di -m
I book -ACC Hasan -DAT Ali -DAT give -CAUS -PAST -1SG

We may say that since the direct object position is already filled in (6b), the causee, i.e. *Häsän* must take the non-direct object position; but this position is already occupied and two NPs can not occur in the non-direct object position in the same clause. Thus, the sentence in (6c) is ungrammatical. However, there is no such a constraint for the syntactic causativisation of the above clauses.

The behaviour of locative, instrumental and benefactive cases is different from the above cases; thus, when there is a locative, an instrumental or a benefactive, the causee can take the position of the dative. Consider the following examples:

7 (a) Häsän kitab -I bag -da goy -du

Hasan(NOM) book -ACC garden -LOC put -PAST.3SG

'Hasan put the book in the garden.'

(b) män kitab -I bag -da goy -dur -du -m

I book -ACC garden -LOC put -CAUS -PAST -1SG

'I made (someone) put the book in the garden.'

(c) män kitab -I Häsän -yä bag -da goy -dur -du -m

I book -ACC Hasan -DAT garden -LOC put -CAUS -PAST -1SG

'I made Hasan put the book in the garden.'

8 (a) Häsän kitab -I Ali -ichin oxu -du

Hasan(NOM) book -ACC Ali -BEN read -PAST.3SG

'Hasan read the book for Ali.'

(b) män kitab -I Ali -ichin oxu -t -du -m

I book -ACC Ali -BEN read -CAUS -PAST -1SG

'I made (someone) read the book for Ali.'

(c) män kitab -I Häsän -yä Ali -ichin oxu -t -du -m

I book -ACC Hasan -DAT Ali -BEN read -CAUS -PAST -1SG

'I made Hasan read the book for Ali.'

9 (a) Häsän kitab -I mIdad -Inan yaz -dI
Hasan(NOM) book -ACC pencil -
INST write -PAST.3SG 'Hasan wrote the book with the pencil.'

(b) män kitab -I mIdad -Inan yaz -dIr -dI -m
I book -ACC pencil -INST write -CAUS -PAST -1SG
'I made (someone) write the book with the pencil.'

(c) män kitab -I Häsän -yä mIdad -Inan yaz -dIr -dI -m
I book -ACC Hasan -DAT pencil -INST write -CAUS-PAST -1SG
'I made Hasan write the book with the pencil.'

As we see in the above sentences, since the NP is in the locative case in (7), in the benefactive case in (8) and in the instrumental case in (9), the causee i.e. *Häsän* can occupy the dative position in the causative clause.

3.1.5.2 A constraint on the causativisation of lexical verbs

There is another constraint on the morphological causative construction of Azeri: when there is a lexical causative counterpart for a verb, it cannot be causativised by affixing the causative morpheme. This sort of lexical causative verb is not morphologically related to the non-causative verb. However, there are only a few verbs which have a lexical counterpart, and hence can not be causativised morphologically. These verbs are:

/gäl/	'come!'	/gätir/	'bring!'	* /gäl-dir/
/get/	'go!'	/apar/	'take!'	* /get-dir/
/gör/	'see!'	/görsät/	'show!'	* /gör-dür/

Interestingly, these lexical causatives can themselves be causativised by affixing the causative morpheme, as illustrated below:

/gätir/	'bring!'	/gätir-t/	'make someone bring it'
/apar/	'take!'	/apar-t/	'make someone take it'
/görsät/	'show!'	/görsät-dir/	'make someone show it'

However, all the above verbs have syntactic causative counterparts.

Morphological causativisation in Azeri, is blocked by passivisation; that is, when the verbis in the passive form, it can not be causativised, as shown below:

/ich/	'drink!'	/ich-il/	'be drunk'	* /ich-il-dir/
/vlr/	'beat!'	/vlr-Il/	'be beaten'	* /vlr-Il-dlr/
/yaz/	**'write!'**	**/yaz-Il/**	**'be written'**	*** /yaz-Il-dlr/**

3.2.6 Double causatives

In Azeri, two causative suffixes can be affixed to verb stems sequentially to form double causatives. Consider the following examples:

/gech/ 'pass!' /gech-irt/ 'make him pass' /gech-irt-dir/ 'make someone make him pass'

/gach/ 'run!' /gach-Irt/ 'make him run' /gach-Irt-dIr/ 'make someone make him run'

/yey/ 'eat!' /yey-dirt/ 'make him eat' /yey-dirt-dir/ 'make someone make him eat'

/Ich/ 'drink!' /ich-irt/ 'make him drink' /ich-irt-dir/ 'make someone make him drink'

/yat/ 'sleep!' /yat-Irt/ 'make him sleep' /yat-Irt-dIr/ 'make someone make him sleep'

/išlä/ 'work!' /išlä-t/ 'make him work' /išlä-t-dIr/ 'make someone make him work'

The encoding of the causer and causee in the double causative construction is illustrated by the following sentences:

10 (a) at gach-dI
horse (NOM) run -PAST.3SG

'The horse ran.'

(b) Ali at -I gach -Irt -dI
Ali (NOM) horse -ACC run -CAUS -PAST.3SG

'Ali made the horse run.'

(c) män at -I Ali -yä gach -Irt -dIr -dI -m
I horse -ACC Ali -DAT run -CAUS -CAUS -PAST -1SG

'I made Ali make the horse run.'

11 (a) mašIn išlä -di
machine (NOM) work -PAST.3SG

'The machine worked.'

(b) Ali mašIn -I išlä -t -di
Ali (NOM) machine -ACC work -CAUS -PAST.3SG

'Ali made the machine work.'

(c) män mašIn -I Ali -yä išlä -t -dir -di -m
I machine -ACC Ali -DAT work -CAUS -CAUS -PAST -1SG

'I made Ali make the machine work.'

The causee, *Ali*, can be omitted from the double causative sentences in (10c) and (11c):

12 män at -I gach -Irt -dIr -dI -m
I horse -ACCrun -CAUS -CAUS -PAST -1SG

'I made (some one)[35] make the horse run.'

13 män mašIn -I išlä -t -dir -di -m
I machine -ACC work -CAUS -CAUS -PAST -1SG

'I made (some one) make the machine work.'

In (12) and (13), though the causee has been deleted, double causativity is still conveyed. However, if we omit the second causative suffix, i.e. /dIr/ from these sentences, they will still be grammatical, but no longer convey the double causative meaning.

There is a constraint on double causativisation: ditransitive verbs can not undergo such a process, as shown below:

---

[35] This omitted causee can also be translated as 'something' when it is an inanimate NP.

/ver/	'give!'	/ver-dir/	'make him give'	* /ver-dir-t/
/al/	'get!'	/al-dlr/	'make him get'	* /al-dlr-t/

3.2.7 Causativisation of compound verbs

In Persian, there are a huge number of compound verbs which are formed by a noun or an adjective followed by an auxiliary verb like /šo/ 'become!' and /kon/ 'do!' (see section 2.10.1.7). Compound verbs with the auxiliary verb /šo/ are in the non-causative form, and those with the auxiliary /kon/ are their corresponding causatives. Some examples are:

/sävar šo/	'get on!'	/sävar kon/	'make someone get on'
/bidar šo/	'wake up!'	/bidar kon/	'make someone wake up'
/gärm šo/	'heat!'	/gärm kon/	'make someone heat'

Azeri has borrowed some of these compound verbs, by retaining the noun or adjective component and changing the auxiliary to a native equivalent (e.g. /än/ 'get off!'). The same strategy as in Persian is followed to causativise these verbs, as illustrated by the following examples:

/xarab ol/	'be destroyed'	/xarab elä/	'destroy!'
/piyadä	'get off!'	/piyadä elä/	'make

ol/ someone get off'
/pak ol/ 'be clean!' /pak elä/ 'make it clean'

These borrowed verbs are used by those who have completed at least primary school, and the number of such verbs is increasing, in spite of the existence of corresponding non-compound native verbs. They are gradually replacing their equivalent native verbs in the conversation of those people who have not had at least a primary school education, too, especially in those provinces where Persian is the main language.

3.2.8 **The interaction between causativisation and passivisation**

In Azeri, the passive suffix /Il/ is affixed to the verb stem to passivise it (see section 2.5.2):

14 (a) Ali mašIn -I gara⍰-da goy -du
Ali (NOM) car -ACC garage -LOC put -PAST.3SG
'Ali put the car in the garage.'

(b) mašin (Ali -nin väsilä -si -inän) car (NOM) (Ali -GEN.3SG means -POSS.3SG -INST) gara⍰ -da goy -ul -du
garage -LOC put -PASS -PAST.3SG
'The car was put in the garage (by Ali).'

A causativisation paradigm follows:

15 (a) Ali alma -nI yey -di
Ali (NOM) apple -ACC eat -PAST.3SG

'Ali ate the apple.'

(b) män bayls ol -du -m (ki) Ali alma -nI yey -yä

I cause -PAST -1SG (COMP) Ali (NOM) apple -ACC eat-SUBJ.3SG

'I caused Ali to eat the apple.'

16 (a) alma yey -il -di
apple (NOM) eat -PASS -PAST.3SG

'The apple was eaten.'

(b) män bayls ol -du -m (ki) alma yey -il -yä

I cause -PAST -1SG (COMP) apple (NOM) eat -PASS -SUBJ.3SG

'I caused the apple to be eaten.'

The sentence in (15b) is the result of syntactic causativisation of the sentence in (15a). In (16b), the passive clause is causativised syntactically as an embedded clause.

Furthermore, in Azeri, causativisation and passivisation can not co-occur morphologically, as illustrated by the ungrammatical sentence in (17d):

17 (a) Ali alma -nI yey -di
Ali (NOM) apple -ACC eat -PAST.3SG
'Ali ate the apple.'

(b) alma yey -il -di
apple (NOM) eat -PASS -PAST.3SG
'The apple was eaten.'

(c) män alma -nI Ali -yä yey -dirt -di -m
I apple -ACC Ali -DAT eat -CAUS -PAST -1SG
'I made Ali eat the apple.'

(d) * alma Ali -yä yey -dirt -il -di
apple (NOM) Ali -DAT eat -CAUS -PASS -PAST.3SG

(e) * Ali alma -nI yey -dirt -il -di
Ali (NOM) apple -ACC eat -CAUS -PASS -PAST.3SG

(f) * Ali -yä alma -nI yey -dirt -il -di
Ali -DAT apple -ACC eat -CAUS -PASS -PAST.3SG

3.2 Embedded clauses

Embedded clauses in Azeri will be discussed under two sub-headings: complement clauses and adjunct clauses.

3.2.1 Complement clauses

Typologically, Azeri has a four-member system of complement clauses: (I) infinitive, (II) indicative, (III) subjunctive, and (IV) optative. We will discuss each of these complementtypes in the following sections.

3.2.1.1 Infinitive complement clauses

In this type, the verb in the complement clause is in the infinitive form and is in a possession relation with the subject of the clause, where the subject is the possessor and the verb is nominalised by taking a case suffix and functions as the possessed entity. Thistype is a nominalised complement which has the internal structure of noun phrases. That is, the predicate assumes the form of a verbal noun and functions as the head noun of the noun phrase. Consider the following example:

30 män ušag -In gäl -mäx -i -ni ešit -di -m
I child -GEN.3SG come -INFI -POSS.3SG -ACC hear -PAST -1SG

'I heard that the child came.'

As we see in (30), the complement clause occurs between the subject and the verb of the matrix clause. The subject of the complement clause, /ušag/ 'child' carries a genitive suffix and the verb, /gäl/ 'come!', is in the infinitive form. The possessive suffix is affixed to this verb and is followed by the accusative case suffix.

When the embedded verb is infinitive, it is not clear whether the action specified by the verb has occured in the past or in the non past, as in:

31 Ali män -im get -mäx -im -i ešit -di
Ali I -GEN.1SG go -INFI -POSS.1SG -ACC hear -PAST.3SG

'Ali heard that I will go/went/am going.'

In (31), it is not clear whether the action of *going* has occurred in the past, present, or future. This tense ambiguity is resolved within context. For example, if the speaker first says:

32 män sabah get -

yäjäx -äm I tomorrow
go -FUT -1SG 'I will go
tomorrow.'

the listener knows that the action in the embedded clause in (32) will take place in the future.

Sometimes, the complement clause does not contain a possession relation, and it simply allows a case suffix, as illustrated in the following example:

33 (a) mäšrub ich -mäx Ali -ni mäst elä -di
alcoholdrink -INFI Ali -ACC drunk do -PAST.3SG
'Drinking alcohol made Ali drunk.'

(b) män mäšrub ich -mäx-i gadagan elä -di -m
I alcoholdrink -INFI -ACC forbidden do -PAST -1SG
'I forbade drinking alcohol.'

In (33a), the complement /mäšrub ichmäx/ 'drinking alcohol' is in the subject position which takes the nominative case, and in (33b), it is the object which takes an accusative case. As we see, there is no possession relation within these clauses, unlike the clause in (31).

Noonan (1985:108) calls complements like those in (33) 'activity or state nominalisations' which "refer to kinds of activities or states, not to specific events or states constituting backgrounded information". On the other hand, he refers to complements like in (31) as 'nominalised propositions' which "are used by speakers to refer to information given previously in a discourse or taken as background to a discourse".

3.2.1.2 Indicative complement clauses

In this type, the complement clause occurs after an optional complementiser, /ki/, which is preceded by the matrix verb. Consider this example:

34   män ešit -di-m (ki) ušag gäl -di
I hear -PAST -1SG COMP child come -PAST.3SG

'I heard that the child came.'

In (34), the complement clause has a finite verb which is inflected for tense and person.

In Azeri, unlike in English which has rules for sequences of tense, the indicative complement clause does not necessarily have the same tense as the main clause, and it could have a tense different from that of the matrix clause, as in:

35 (a) Ali bil -di (ki) män get -ir -äm
Ali (NOM) know -PAST.3SG COMP I go - CONT.NPAST -1SG
'Ali found out that I was going.'

(b) Ali bil -ir (ki) män get -di -m
Ali (NOM) know -NPAST.CONT.3SG COMP I go -PAST -1SG 'Ali knows that I went.'

In (35a), the embedded verb is in the present tense and continuous aspect, while the main verb is in the past tense. Similarly, in (35b), the embedded verb is in the past tense, although the main verb is in the non-past tense.

3.2.1.3 Subjunctive complement clauses

In this type, the verb in the complement clause takes a subjunctive suffix, /yA/. The occurrence of the complementiser /ki/ is also optional in this form:

36 män istä -di-m (ki) ušag gäl -yä
I ask -PAST -1SG COMP child come -SUBJ.3SG
'I asked the child to come.'

In (36), the embedded verb contains the subjunctive suffix /yA/, which was discussed in section 1.1.2.5. This suffix exhibits the person and number agreement, and when there is a word like /šayäd/ 'may' or /gäräk/ 'should' in the clause, it inflects for copular tense. The subjunctive suffix can also convey possibility and obligation when it occurs in the main clause. Consider these examples:

37 (a) šayäd get -yä -äm
may go -SUBJ -NPAST.1SG
'I may go.'

(b) šayäd get -yä -sän
may go -SUBJ -NPAST.2SG
'you may go.'

(c) šayäd get -yä -idi -m
may go -SUBJ -COP.PAST -1SG
'I might have gone[36].'

38 (a) gäräk get -yä -äm

shouldgo -SUBJ -NPAST.1SG

'I should go.'

(b) gäräk get -yä -sän
should go -SUBJ -NPAST.2SG

---

36 Here, since the possibility of *going* is in the past tense, the gloss *might* is used to convey the past tense forthe clause.

'You should go.'

(c) gäräk get -yä -idi -m
should go -SUBJ -
COP.PAST -1SG'I should
have gone.'

39 o gäl -sä män šayäd get -yä -äm
3SG (NOM)come -COND I may go -SUBJ -NPAST.1SG
'If he comes, I may go.'

As we see, the subjunctive takes a past tense in (37c) and (38c) where there is a word like

/šayäd/ 'may' and /gäräk/ 'should'.

There are some pieces of evidence for considering /šayäd/ and /gäräk/[37] as modals:

(I) These two words are not genuine verbs because they do not take any verb endings, and they are not nouns because they do not take a nominal ending, and they are neither adjectives because they can not precede a noun to modify it. Thus, we can regard these words as modals. Moreover, /šayäd/ 'may' which is a borrowed word, was used in old Persian texts as a genuine verb, while in current Persian, it is used only as a modal. (II) When they occur in the subjunctive clause, it is possible for the clause to occur as a main clause. For example in the sentence, /o gäräk gälyä/ 'He should come.', the occurrence of

/gäräk/ makes it possible for the clause to occur as a main clause, while the sentence will be ungrammatical without it, as in */o gälyä/. However, there is no direct evidence for these two words being modals.

The subjunctive suffix /yA/ is in complementary distribution with the conditional suffix

/sA/. That is, the latter occurs within the *if clause* while the former occurs within the *then* clause, as shown in sentence (39). Furthermore, the conditional suffix does not occur within a main clause or clauses which convey possibility, obligation and habituality.

---

[37] However, /gäräk/ 'should' used to take a copular ending in the previous generation' speech, as in: /bu bizä gäräkdi/ 'This is necessary for us.', where /gäräk/ is inflected for non past tense and third person singular.

The subjunctive suffix can occur in head-final complement clauses while the infinitive suffix /mAx/ occurs in head-initial clauses. Secondly, the former only takes copular tense endings and person/number suffixes, while the latter is followed by the possessive and case suffixes. Thirdly, the verb containing /mAx/ can occur in clauses which function as subjects as well as objects, as shown below:

40 (a) yalan dey -mäx chox pis iš -di
lie tell -INFI very bad work -COP.NPAST.3SG
'Lying is very bad.'

(b) män yalan dey -mäx -i gadagan elä -di -m

I lie tell -INFI -ACC forbidden do-PAST -1SG

'I forbade lying.'

On the other hand, the verb containing /yA/ can only occur within a clause which is a complement of the matrix verb as shown in (36). Finally, the verb which takes /mAx/ cannot occur in the main clause, while the verb containing /yA/ can, as we see in (37-38).

There is also a complementary distribution between the subjunctive and optative verb forms, on the one hand, and indicative verb form, on the other: when the verb of the matrix clause is a verb of possibility, obligation, or demand, such as /dey/ 'say!', /istä/ 'ask!', /dästur ver/ 'order!', /yalvar/ 'beg!', the verb of the complement clause occurs as subjunctive or optative; when the verb of the matrix clause does not belong to this class of verbs, the subordinate verb will be indicative.

Noonan (1985:53) states that in classical Greek, the tense distinction is lost in the subjunctive, and aspectual distinctions are neutralised. He also claims (1985:54) that "if the indicative has subject-verb or object-verb agreement, the subjunctive will almost invariably code these categories as well". This generalisation is true in the case of Azeri where both the indicative and the subjunctive exhibit subject-verb agreement.

3.2.1.4 Optative complement clauses[38]

The fourth type of complement clauses is optative where the embedded verb takes an optative ending (see section 2.8), as illustrated below:

41 (a) o istä -di (ki) Ali get -sin
3SG(NOM) ask -PAST.3SG COMP Ali go
-OPT.3SG
'He asked Ali to go.'

(b) o istä -di (ki) män get-yim
3SG(NOM) ask -PAST.3SG COMP I go
-OPT.1SG 'He asked me to go.'

Here, the verb of the complement clause denotes a suggestion or a desire made by the subject of the main clause.

3.2.1.5 The *goy* construction

In this construction the matrix verb which is /goy/ 'let!' is in the imperative or optative

mood and the embedded verb take optative endings, as in:

42 goy māń get -yim
let (IMP.2SG) I go -OPT.1SG

'Let me go.'

The complementiser /ki/ can not precede the complement clause in *goy* construction, while for other types of complement clauses, it is optional:

43 * goy ki mān get -yim
let (IMP.2SG) COMP I go -OPT.1SG

Davies (1986:6) states that in English "the first and third person pronouns which are impossible as imperative subjects can occur in the *let* construction, whereas the *you* subject common in imperatives is excluded from it", as in:

---

[38] In Lee's study (1996), this type of clause is called subjunctive, while they are treated as imperatives in simple clauses.

44 Let me / him / us / them / * you be quite clear about this.

In Azeri, *you* is also possible with the *goy* construction where *goy* takes a first or thirdperson optative morpheme. Consider these examples:

45 (a) goy män bu -nu kamilän anla -ylm
let (IMP.2SG) I this -ACC completely understand -OPT.1SG

'Let me be quite clear about this[39].'

(b) goy o bu -nu kamilän anla -sln
let (IMP.2SG) 3SG (NOM) this -ACC completely understand -OPT.3SG

'Let him be quite clear about this.'

(c) * goy sän bu -nu kamilän anla
let (IMP.2SG) 2SG (NOM) this -ACC completely understand (IMP.2SG)

46 (a) goy-sun män bu -nu kamilän anla -ylm
let -OPT.3SG I this -ACC completely understand -OPT.1SG

'He may let me be quite clear about this.'

(b) goy -sun o bu -nu kamilän anla -sln

let -OPT.3SG 3SG (NOM) this -ACC completely understand -OPT.3SG

'He may let him be quite clear about this.'

(c) goy -sun sän bu -nu kamilän anla
let -OPT.3SG 2SG (NOM) this -ACC completely understand (IMP.2SG)

'He may let you be quite clear about this.'

47 (a) * goy -yummän bu -nu kamilän anla -ylm
let -OPT.1SG I this -ACC completely understand -OPT.1SG

(b) goy -yum o bu -nu kamilän anla -sln
let -OPT.1SG 3SG (NOM) this -ACC completely understand -OPT.3SG

'I may let him be quite clear about this.'

(c) goy -yum sän bu -nu kamilän anla
let -OPT.1SG 2SG (NOM) this -ACC completely understand (IMP.2SG)

'I may let you be quite clear about this.'

As we see, the sentences in (45c) and (47a) are not grammatical. There may be some

pragmatic reason behind this restriction: In (45c), since the verb /goy/ 'let!' contains the second person imperative morpheme (which surfaces as zero), which results in a situation where a person lets himself do something, which pragmatically is odd and the same happens to the sentence in (47a), where the verb has the first person morpheme and the subject of the embedded clause is also the first person pronoun. Therefore, we can say that there is a restriction on the *goy* construction: when both the matrix and embedded clauses have the same subject, the sentence will be ungrammatical.

3.2.1.6 Properties of complement clauses

The complementiser /ki/ is optionally used with the indicative, subjunctive and optative complement clauses but not with the infinitive ones and *goy* construction. This morpheme also functions as a relativiser in head-initial relative clause constructions (see section 3.1.2.2.2).

When the main clause subject is sentential, the embedded verb is always an infinitive, as illustrated below:

48 (a) Ali -nin yalan dey -mäx -i män -i narahat elä -di
Ali-GEN.3SG lietell -INFI -POSS.3SG I -ACC upset
do -PAST.3SG

'Ali's lying made me upset.'

(b) * Ali yalan dey -di män -i narahat elä -di
Ali (NOM) lie tell -PAST.3SG I -ACC upset
do -PAST.3SG

(c) * Ali yalan dey -yä män -i narahat elä -di
Ali (NOM) lie tell -SUB I -ACC upset do -PAST.3SG

(d) * Ali yalan dey -sin män -i narahat elä -di
Ali (NOM) lie tell -OPT.3SG I -ACC upset
do -PAST.3SG

As we see, (48b-d) are ungrammatical because the embedded verb is not infinitive. Adding the complementiser /ki/ to the beginning of these sentences does not rescue them from ungrammaticality. However, in English, the complementiser *that* does:

---

[39] The imperative force here is similar to the *let us* construction in English rather than the *let's* construction. In other words, it implies an order rather than a suggestion.

49 (a) * Ali lied made me upset.
(b) That Ali lied made me upset.

In Azeri, it is possible to move the negative marker from the complement clause to the main clause. This movement is called “negative raising” by Noonan (1985:90). The following examples illustrate such raising:

50 (a) män fikr elä -di -m (ki) Ali Häsän -i
I thought do -PAST -1SG COMP
Ali Hasan -ACCvIr -ma -dI
hit -NEG -PAST.3SG
'I thought that Ali did not hit Hasan.'

(b) män fikr elä -mä -di -m (ki) Ali Häsän -i
I thought do -NEG -PAST -1SG COMP
Ali Hasan -ACCvIr -dI
hit -PAST.3SG
'I did not think that Ali hit Hasan.'

However, this raising is not possible when the main verb is a verb like /pešman ol/ 'regret!':

51 (a) män pešman ol -du -m (ki) Ali Häsän -i

I regretted be -PAST -1SG COMP Ali Hasan -ACCvlr -ma -dI

hit -NEG -PAST.3SG

'I regretted that Ali did not hit Hasan.'

(b) män pešman ol -ma -dI -m (ki) Ali Häsän -i

I regretted be -NEG -PAST -1SG COMP Ali Hasan - ACCvlr -dI

hit -PAST.3SG

'I did not regret that Ali hit Hasan.'

As we see, the sentence in (51b) where the negative marker is raised, although grammatical, is semantically different from the sentence in (51a).

According to Noonan (1985:97), languages which use indicative/subjunctive opposition to distinguish between realis and irrealis frequently do not have tense distinctions for subjunctives. Azeri can be regarded as one of these languages which uses realis modality

for indicative complements, which contain such verbs as /bil/ 'know!', /ehsas elä/ 'feel!',

/fikr elä/ 'think!', /därk elä/ 'realise!', /täsävür elä/ 'imagine!', /dey/ 'say!', /izhar elä/ 'declare!', /e�lam elä/ 'announce!', and irrealis modality for subjunctive complements

,which contain verbs like /šäk elä/ 'doubt!', /bavär elä/ 'believe!', /istä/ 'want!', /dästur ver/ 'order!', /tärjih ver/ 'prefer!', /tosiyä elä/ 'recommend!', /pišnahad elä/ 'propose!'. However, in Azeri, as mentioned earlier, there can be a copular tense distinction available for subjunctives, when the subjunctive clause have a modal.

There are some verbs which only take an indicative complement. These verbs have been called 'aspectual' by Newmeyer (1975:10) and 'phasal' by Longacre (1983:250), because they refer to the phase of an act or state. These verbs are: /bašla/ 'begin!', /idamä ver/ 'continue!', /gurtar/ 'finish!', /saxla/ 'stop!'. The embedded infinitive for these phasal verbs always takes a dative case, as shown below:

52 Ali yey -mäx -yä bašla -dI

Ali (NOM)eat -INFI -DAT begin -PAST.3SG

'Ali began to eat.'

3.2.1.7 Constraints on the selection of complement clauses

There are constraints on the occurrence of indicative, subjunctive and optative verb forms in embedded clauses. The mood of the embedded verb is determined by the type of the matrix verb, as follows:

(I) If the matrix verb is one of the following verbs, the embedded verb will be indicative:

/mä⍰lum ol/ 'appear!', /näzärä gäl/ 'seem!', /gör/ 'see!', /bavär elä/ 'believe!', /bil/ 'know!', /ešit/ 'hear!', /ehsas elä/ 'feel!', /fikr elä/ 'think!', /täsävür elä/ 'imagine!'. We may call these verbs "cognitive". Neither subjunctive nor optative embedded verbs are allowed with these verbs, as shown below:

53 (a) mä⍰lum ol -du (ki) Ali gäl -
yäjäx evident be -PAST.3SG COMP
Ali come -FUT.3SG

'It appeared that Ali would come.'

(b) * mä⍰lum ol -du (ki) Ali gäl -yä
evident be -PAST.3SG COMP Ali come -SUBJ.3SG

(c) * mä⍰lum ol -du (ki) Ali gäl -sin
evident be -PAST.3SG COMP Ali come -OPT.3SG

However, if we include a modal like /šayäd/ 'may', or /gäräk/ 'should' in the embedded clause, it is possible for this clause to be subjunctive. For example the sentence in (53b) can be grammatical by adding the modal /gäräk/ 'should':

54 mä⍰lum ol -du (ki) Ali gäräk gäl -yä
evident be -PAST.3SG COMP Ali should come -SUBJ.3SG

'It appeared that Ali had to come.'

These modals can occur in the embedded clause when the matrix verb implies possibility, but not certainty. For example, they can occur with the verb /mä⍰lum ol/ 'appear!', but not with the verb /gör/ 'see!'.

(II) If the matrix verb is among the following verbs, the embedded verb will only be in the subjunctive form: /tärjih ver/ 'prefer!', /šäk elä/ 'doubt!', /ijazä ver/ 'allow!', as illustrated below:

55 (a) Ali tärjih ver -di (ki) gäl -yä
Ali (NOM) preference give -PAST.3SG COMP come -SUBJ.3SG

'Ali prefered to come.'

(b) * Ali tärjih ver -di (ki) gäl -yäjäx
Ali (NOM) preference give -PAST.3SG COMP come -FUT.3SG

(c) * Ali tärjih ver -di (ki) gäl -sin
Ali (NOM) preference give -PAST.3SG COMP come -OPT.3SG

(I) If the matrix verb belongs to the following group of verbs, the embedded verb can be either in subjunctive or in optative form: /dey/ 'say!', /talaš elä/ 'try!', /vadar elä/ 'force!', /israr elä/ 'insist!', /istä/ 'ask!', /xahiš elä/ 'request!', /pišnahad elä/

'suggest!', /tosiyä elä/ 'recommend!', /dästur ver/, 'order!'. Consider these

examples:

56 (a) män dästur ver -di -m (ki) Ali gäl -yä
I order give - PAST - 1SG COMP Ali come - SUBJ.3SG
'I ordered Ali to come.'

(b) män dästur ver -di -m (ki) Ali gäl -sin
I order give - PAST - 1SG COMP Ali come - OPT.3SG
'I ordered Ali to come.'

(c) * män dästurver -di -m (ki) Ali gäl -di
I order give - PAST - 1SG COMP Ali come - PAST.3SG

As we see, (56c) is ungrammatical because when the matrix verb is a verb like /dästur

ver/ 'order!', the embedded verb can not be in the indicative form.

There is a semantic distinction between optative and subjunctive embedded clauses in this group: when the embedded verb is in the optative form, as in (56b), the probability of its occurrence is higher than that of the subjunctive form, as in (56a). For example, the action of *coming* in (56b) is more likely than in (56a). It also seems that the obligation behind the action in (56b) is greater than that of (56a).

3.2.2 Adjunct clauses

There are two types of adjunct clauses: (I) adverbial clauses, and (II) relative clause constructions. Both types will be discussed in this section.

3.2.2.1 Adverbial clauses

In Azeri, there are three types of adverbial clauses. The first type is formed by affixing the participial suffix /yAn/ to the verb which is followed by either the locative case suffix,

/dA/, or the ablative case suffix, /dAn/, as illustrated below:

57 (a) sän gäl -yän -dä män get -di -m

2SG (NOM) come -PRT -LOC I go -PAST -1SG

'I went when you came.'

(b) sän gäl -yän -dän sonra män get -di -m
2SG (NOM) come -PRT -ABL after I go
-PAST -1SG 'I went after you came.'

As we see in (57b), the ablative case suffix /dAn/ is used, followed by the postposition

/sonra/ 'after'.

In the second type, the participial suffix /yenjA/ is affixed to the verb of the adverbial clause, as shown below:

58 sän gäl -yenjä män get -di -m
2SG (NOM) come -PRT I go -
PAST -1SG 'I went before you came.'

There is a difference between the time of /gäl/ 'come!' in (57a) and (58). In the former, the act of *coming* in the adverbial clause and the act of *going* in the main clause take place simultaneously, while in the latter, *going* takes place just before *coming*.

The third type of adverbial clauses is formed by adding the participial suffix /dIg/ to the verb which is followed by the suffix /-jA/ 'as long as (time)':

59 sän oxu -dug -ja män yaz -dI
-m 2SG (NOM) read -PRT -as long as I
write -PAST -1SG 'I wrote as long as you
read.'

Embedded clauses in Azeri exhibit the same constituent order as simple sentences; that is, the verb is the final constituent of the clause.

There are two possible analysis for /yenjä/ in (58): it consists of two separate morphemes,

i. e. /yän/ and /jä/, or it is a single morpheme. If we consider the first possibility, where

/yen/ is regarded the same as /yän/ participial with a phonological change of /ä/ to /e/. In this case, its second morpheme /jä/ will be similar to /jä/ suffix following the participial

/dig/.

However, if we consider /yen/ as the participial, then its meaning in combination with /jä/ should be similar to that of the other participial /dig-jä/. But as we see in (60b) and (60c), their meanings are different from each other:

60 (a) sän gäl -yän -dä män get -di -m
2SG (NOM) come -PRT -LOC I go .
-PAST -1SG
'I went when you came.'

(b) sän gäl -yenjä män get -di -m
2SG (NOM) come -PRT I go -
PAST -1SG 'I went as soon as you
came.'

(c) sän gäl -dig -jä män get -di -m
2SG (NOM) come -PRT -as long as I go
-PAST -1SG 'I went as long as you came.'

Another problem for this analysis is that there is no environment where /ä/ in the participial /yän/ can change into /e/ and surfaces as /yen/.

Therefore, we should consider the second analysis where /-enjä/ is a single morpheme which expresses a time reference for the occurrence of the action of the main verb before that of the embedded verb.

In adverbial clauses, the verb does not inflect for tense, and its tense is interpreted from that of the matrix verb. For example, in (57), the tense of the embedded clause is interpreted as past because the matrix verb is in the past tense. The embedded verb does neither inflect for person/number, and hence the subject of the subordinate clause, unlike that of the main clause, can not be deleted. For example, if we delete the subject of the embedded clause in (57), it will result in the ungrammaticality of the sentence, as in (61):

61 * gäl -yän -dä män get -di -m
come -PRT -LOC I go -PAST -
1SG

3.2.2.2 Relative clause constructions

There are two types of relative clause in Azeri. The first type is head-final where the relative clause precedes the head noun and a relativiser suffix is affixed to the verb. The second type is head-initial where the relative clause follows the head noun and is preceded by a morphologically invariant relativiser. This type is borrowed from Persian. In the following sections, we discuss each of these constructions separately; then, we examine the possible constraints on each of them.

3.2.2.2.1 Head-final relative clause constructions

In this type, one of the relativiser suffixes, i.e. /yAn/ or /dIg/[40] is affixed to the verb of the relative clause which precedes the head. Since these relativisers behave differently, we will discuss them separately. First, consider the following example involving the relativiser /yAn/:

62 (a) kiši at -I sür -dü
man(NOM) horse -ACC
ride -PAST.3SG 'The
man rode the horse.'

63

(b) at -I sür -yän kiši get -di

horse -ACC ride -REL man go -PAST.3SG

'The man who was riding the horse went.'

(c) kiši sür -yän at get -di

man ride -REL horse go -PAST.3SG

'The horse which was ridden by the man went.'

The relativiser suffix /yAn/ replaces the tense, aspect, and person/number suffixes. That is, the verb in the relative clause has no tense, aspect, or agreement, and so it is not possible to determine the tense and aspect of the relative clause out of context. For example, the relative clause in (62b) can be interpreted either as 'the man who was riding' or 'the man who is riding'. However, the preferred interpretation of its tense and

---

[40] These two suffixes can also function as participial (see section 1.1.2.6).

aspect is the same as the matrix clause, e.g. when the matrix verb is in the past tense, the relativised verb is also interpreted as having the past tense.

As we see in (62), in this type of relative clause, the head noun occurs after the relativised verb. In other words, the only change in the constituent order is that the head is postverbal. Now we turn to the second relativiser, /dIg/. Consider the following examples:63 (a) kiši at -I sür - dü

man(NOM) horse -ACC ride -PAST.3SG

'The man rode the horse.'

(b) kiši -nin sür -düg -ü at get -di

man -GEN.3SG ride -REL -POSS.3SG horse go -PAST.3SG

'The horse which was ridden by the man went.'

Here also the relativiser suffix /dlg/ is affixed to the verb root, /sür/ 'ride!', which occurs before the head. Additionally, there is a possession relation between the subject, /kiši/ 'man', and this verb. That is, when /dlg/ is affixed to the verb, it is followed by a possessive suffix which agrees in person and number with the subject of the relative clause.

There is a constraint on using this type of the relative clause: objects but not subjects can be relativised in this way. On the other hand, the first type can relativise both NPs, as illustrated by the following examples:

64 (a) ušag alma -nl yey -ir
child(NOM) apple -ACC eat -CONT.NPAST.3SG

'The child is eating the apple.'

(b) ušag yey -yän alma širin -di
child eat -REL apple sweet -COP.NPAST.3SG

'The apple which is eaten by the child is sweet.'

(c) ušag -In yey -dig -i alma širin -di
child -GEN.3SG eat -REL -POSS.3SG apple sweet -
COP.NPAST.3SG

'The apple which is eaten by the child is sweet.'

(d) alma -nl yey -yän ušag gäl -ir
apple -ACC eat -REL child come -CONT.NPAST.3SG

'The child who eats the apple is coming.'

(e)* alma -nln yey -dig -i ušag gäl-ir
apple -GEN.3SG eat -REL -POSS.3SG child come -CONT.NPAST.3SG

As we see in (64), /yAn/ can relativise both object and subject, but /dlg/ relativises only the object. However, it seems that only complements can be relativised by /dlg/ and not adjuncts, as illustrated below:

65 (a) Ali bag -ya yetiš -di
Ali garden -DAT reach -PAST.3SG

'Ali reached the garden.'

(b) Ali yetiš -yän bag
Ali reach -REL
garden 'the garden
which Ali reached'

(c) Ali -nin yetiš -dig -i bag
Ali -GEN.3SG reach -REL -
POSS.3SG garden 'the garden which
Ali reached'

66 (a) Ali bag -dan chlx -dl
Ali garden -ABL come out -PAST.3SG

'Ali came out of the garden.'

(b) Ali chlx -yan bag
Ali come out-REL
garden 'the garden
where Ali came out of'

(c) Ali -nin chlx -dlg -l bag
Ali -GEN.3SG come out -REL -
POSS.3SG garden'the garden where Ali
came out of'

67 (a) Ali bag -da gal -dl
Ali garden -LOC stay -PAST.3SG
'Ali stayed in the garden.'

(b) Ali gal -yan bag
Ali stay -REL
garden

'the garden where Ali stayed'

(c) * Ali -nin gal -dlg -l bag
Ali -GEN.3SG stay -REL
-POSS.3SG garden

68 (a) Ali kitab -Ichln gäz
-di
Ali book -BEN search -PAST.3SG
'Ali searched for the
book.'

(b) Ali gäz -yän
kitabAli search -
REL book
'the book which Ali searched for'

(c) * Ali -nin gäz -dig -i
kitabAli -GEN.3SG search -
REL -POSS.3SG book

As we see in (65) and (66), both /yAn/ and /dIg/ can be used to relativise a non-direct object, i.e. a complement, but only /yAn/ can be used to construct a relative clause involving an adjunct, e.g. the NP in the locative case in (67), or the NP in the benefactivecase in (68).

When the head noun is a possessor within a subject NP, it can still be relativised only by

/yAn/, and not by /dIg/:

69 (a) gIz -In sach -I uzun -du
girl -GEN.3SG hair -POSS.3SG long -COP.NPAST.3SG
'The girl's hair is long.'

(b) sach -I uzun -ol -yan gIz gäl -ir
hair -POSS.3SG long -become -REL girl
come -CONT.NPAST.3SG

'The girl whose hair is long is coming.'

(c) * sach -I uzun -ol -dug -u gIz gäl -ir
hair -POSS.3SG long-become -REL -POSS.3SG girl come-
CONT.NPAST.3SG

As we see in (69c), though /gIz/ 'girl' is the possessor of /sach/ 'hair' within the subject, the suffix /dIg/ cannot be used.

However, when the head noun is a possessor within an NP in the object position, it can be relativised by either /yAn/ or /dIg/:

70 (a) sänglz -In sach -I -nI istä -ir -sän
you girl GEN.3SG hair -POSS.3SG -ACC like -
CONT.NPAST -2SG 'You like the girl's hair.'

(b) sän sach -I -nI istä -yan
glzyou hair -POSS.3SG -ACC like
-REL girl 'the girl whose hair you like'

(c) sän sach -I -nI istä -dig -in
glz you hair -POSS.3SG -ACC like -REL -
POSS.2SG girl 'the girl whose hair you like'

In (70), since the possessor, /gIz/ 'girl' is within the NP in object position, it can be relativised by both /yAn/ as in (70b) and /dIg/ as in (70c).

When the subject is a pronoun, it can occur with or without a genitive case, as illustrated in (71):

71 (a) sän -in istä -dig -in glz
you -GEN.2SG like -REL -
POSS.2SG girl 'the girl whom you like'

(b) sän istä -dig -in
gl
zyou like -REL -POSS.2SG
girl 'the girl whom you like'

However, the deletion of the genitive suffix is not possible when the subject is a noun, as we see in the ungrammatical sentence in (72b):

72 (a) Ali -nin istä -dig-i
glz Ali -GEN.3SG
like -REL -POSS.3SG
girl 'the girl whom Ali likes'

(b) * Ali istä -dig -i
gl
z Ali like -REL -POSS.3SG
girl

There is a constraint on the occurrence of the subject in the genitive case: when the head noun is a possessor, the subject can not occur in this case; otherwise the sentence will be ungrammatical as we see in (73b):

73 (a) Ali sach -I -nI istä -dig-i gIz
Ali hair -POSS.3SG -ACC like -REL -
POSS.3SG girl'the girl whose hair Ali likes'

(b) * Ali -nin sach -I -nI istä -dig -i
gIz Ali -GEN.3SG hair -POSS.3SG -ACC like -REL
-POSS.3SG girl

In (73b), since the head noun, /gIz/ 'girl', is the possessor of /sach/ 'hair', the subject, *Ali*, can not occur in the genitive case.

When /dIg/ is used to relativise non-subject NPs, since there is an agreement marker on the possessive suffix, it is possible to delete the subject. For example, if we delete the subject in (74a), it will still be grammatical:

74 (a) män gör -düg -
üm kiši I see -REL -
POSS.1SG man'the man
whom I saw'

(b) gör -düg -
üm kiši see -REL
-POSS.1SG
man 'the man
whom I saw'

However, when /yAn/ is used to relativise the noun that heads non-subject NPs, there is no such agreement marker to recover the subject and hence the presence of the subject is obligatory. For example, if we delete the subject in (75a), it will be ungrammatical:

75 (a) män gör -yän
ki
ši I see -REL
man 'the man
whom I saw'

(b) * gör
-yän
kiši
see -
REL
man

At first glance, it seems that Azeri allows relativisation out of sentential subjects:

76 (a) kiši -nin oyan -max -I chox chätin -di

man -GEN.3SG wake -INFI -POSS.3SG very difficult -COP.NPAST.3SG

'It is very difficult for the man to wake up.'

(b) oyan -max -I chox chätin ol -yan kiši oyan -dI

wake -INFI -POSS.3SG very difficult become -REL man wake -PAST.3SG

'The man whose waking up was difficult, woke up.'

In fact, (69b) is a closely parallel relative clause construction to (76b) where the head (e.g, /gIz/ 'girl') has a possessive relation with the possessed entity (e.g, /sach/ 'hair'). The difference is that in (76b), the possessed entity appears as a clause, /oynamaxI/.

In the context of infinitival clauses, a further possibility arises: Relativisation out of non- subject infinitival clauses is possible, as illustrated by the following sentences:

77 (a) Ali alma -nI yey -mäx -yä bašla -dI
Ali apple -ACC eat -INFI -DAT begin -PAST.3SG

'Ali began to eat the apple.'

(b) Ali -nin yey -mäx -yä bašla -dlg -I
alma Ali GEN.3SG eat -INFI -DAT
begin -REL -POSS.3SG apple 'the apple which Ali began to eat'

However, when infinitival clauses have a benefactive or an instrumental suffix, they are islands, as shown below:

78 (a) Ali ev -i al -max -Ichln pul ylg -dI
Ali (NOM) house -ACC buy -INFI -BEN money save -PAST.3SG
'Ali saved money to buy the house.'

(b) * Ali -nin al -max -Ichln pul ylg -dlg -I ev Ali -GEN.3SG buy -INFI -BEN money save -REL -POSS.3SG house

79 (a) Ali bag -da išlä -mäx -inän pul ylg -dI
Ali (NOM) garden -LOC work -INFI -INST money save -PAST.3SG
'Ali saved money by working in the garden.'

(b) * Ali -nin išlä -mäx -inän pul ylg -dlg -I bag Ali -GEN.3SG work -INFI -INST money save -REL -POSS.3SG garden

3.2.2.2.2 Head-initial relative clause constructions

In this construction, the relative clause is preceded by the relativiser /ki/, and occurs afterthe head noun, as illustrated by the following examples:

80 (a) o kiši ki män dünän gör -düm bügün get -di
that man REL I yesterday see -PAST.1SG today go -PAST.3SG
'The man whom I saw yesterday left today.'

(b) o kiši ki dünän gäl -miš -di bügün get -di
that man REL yesterday come -ASP -PAST.3SG today go -PAST.3SG
'The man who had come yesterday left today.'

Clearly, we can use the relativiser /ki/ to relativise both an object NP (as in 80a) and a subject NP (as in 80b). As we see in (80), unlike in the head-final construction, the verb has tense, aspect, and agreement.

There is a difference between head-initial and head-final relative clauses: in the former, a determiner occurs before the head, whereas in the latter, there is no determiner, as shown in the following examples:

81 (a) o kitab ki sän oxu -du -n
that book REL you
read -PAST -2SG 'the book
which you read'

(b) sän oxu -yan kitab
2SG(NOM) read -REL
book 'the book which
you read'

Head-initial relative clauses modify only fully specified, definite NPs, while head-final ones can modify any NP:

82 (a) o kiši ki get -di
that man RELgo -PAST.3SG
'the man who went'

(b) * kišiki get -di
man REL go -PAST.3SG

83 (a) o get -yän
kiši that go -REL
man 'the man
who went'

(b) get -yänkiši
go -REL
ma
n 'the man
who went'

In (83a), /o/ 'that' has more demonstrative force than in (82a). In other words, in (82a),

/o/ is just a determiner, whereas in (83a) it involves both the

determiner and the demonstrative meanings.

When there is an adjective, it always occurs adjacent to

the head as we see in (84): 84 (a) o uja kiši

ki get -di

that tall man REL go -PAST.3SG
'the tall man who went'

(b) o get -yän uja kiši
that go -REL tall
man 'the tall man
who went'

In Azeri, both head-final and head-initial relative clauses can co-occur in a sentence. Thus, there can be two relative clauses modifying the same head. In such constructions, the head-final relative clause, i.e. with /yAn/ or /dIg/, occurs before the head, and the head-initial relative clause occurs after the same head, as shown by the following sentences:

85 o gäl -yän kiši ki sän gör -dü -n müdür -dü
that come -REL man REL you see -PAST -2SG manager -COP.NPAST.3SG

'The man who came, whom you saw is a manager.'

86 gör -düg -ün kiši ki alma yey -ir -di
see -REL -POSS.2SG man REL apple eat -CONT -PAST.3SG aj -Idl

hungry-COP.PAST.3SG

'The man whom you saw who was eating the apple was hungry.'

In (86), since the head-final relative clause modifies the head noun, /kiši/ 'man', there is no need for the determiner, /o/ 'that'. For example, in (80b), we can replace /o/ with the head-final relative clause.

It is also possible for a head-final relative clause having the relativiser /yAn/ to co-occur with a relative clause which has the relativiser /dIg/:

87 män -im gör -düg -üm gäl -yän
kišiI -GEN.1SG see -REL -POSS.1SG come
-REL man 'the man whom I saw, who was coming'

88

3.2.2.2.3 **Further properties of relativisation: Resumptive pronouns**

In Azeri, it is possible to relativise a noun within an embedded question, as illustrated below:

89 (a) män bil -mä -ir -äm (ki) kim o
I know -NEG -CONT -NPAST.1SG COMP
who thatalma -lar -I yey -di

apple -PL -ACC eat -PAST.3SG

'I do not know who ate the apples.'

(b) o alma -lar ki män bil -mä -ir -äm

that apple -PL REL I know -NEG -CONT -NPAST.1SG(ki) kim (olar -I)
yey -di

(COMP) who (3PL -ACC) eat -PAST.3SG

'the apples that I do not know who ate (them)'

As we see in (88b), the occurrence of the complementiser, /ki/, and the pronoun, /olar/, is optional; thus, there can be four different options for this sentence, which are illustrated below according to the order of preference of native speakers:

90 (a) o alma-lar ki män bil-mä-ir-äm kim olar-lyey-di
(b) o alma-lar ki män bil-mä-ir-äm kim yey-di
(c) o alma-lar ki män bil-mä-ir-äm ki kim olar-l yey-di
(d) o alma-lar ki män bil-mä-ir-äm ki kim yey-di

However, this type of relativisation is not possible using the head-final construction.

It is worth exploring the behaviour of resumptive pronouns a little further. In Azeri, when the head noun is the subject or direct object, a co-referential pronoun can not occur in the relative clause:

91 (a) o kiši ki män -i gör -dü
that man REL 1SG -ACC see -PAST.3SG
'the man who saw me'

(b) * o kiši ki o män -i gör -dü
that man REL 3SG(NOM) 1SG -ACC see -PAST.3SG

92 (a) o kiši ki män gör -du -m
that man REL I see -PAST -
1SG 'the man whom I saw'

(b) * o kiši ki män on -u gör -du -m
that man REL I 3SG -ACC
see -PAST -1SG

However, when the head noun is a non-direct object (e.g. it is in the dative or ablative case), the pronoun is optional:

93 (a) o kiši ki kitab -I ver -di -m
that man REL book -ACC give -PAST
-1SG 'the man whom I gave the book'

(b) o kiši ki kitab -I on -ya ver -di -m
that man REL book -ACC 3SG -DAT give -
PAST -1SG 'the man whom I gave the book'

94 (a) o bag ki män chIx -dI -m
that garden REL I come out
-PAST -1SG 'the garden which I
came out of'

(b) o bag ki män or -dan chIx -dI -m
that garden REL I there -ABL come out
-PAST -1SG 'the garden which I came out of'

When the head is in the locative, benefactive or instrumental case, (that is, when it is an adjunct) the presence of the pronoun is obligatory, as we see in the following sentences:

95 (a) o bag ki män or -da gal -dI -m
that garden REL I there -LOC stay -
PAST -1SG 'the garden where I stayed'

(b) * o bag ki män gal-dI -
m that garden REL I
stay -PAST -1SG

95 (a) o kiši ki män on -uchun get -di -m
that man REL I 3SG -BEN go -PAST -1SG
'the man whom I went for'

(b) * o kiši ki män get -di -m
that man REL I go
-PAST -1SG

96 (a) o mIdad ki män on -unan yaz -dI -m
that pencil REL I 3SG -INST write -PAST -1SG
'the pencil which I wrote with'

(b) * o mIdad ki män yaz -dI -
m that pencil REL I
write -PAST -1SG

Based on the above examples, we can say that a resumptive pronoun can not occur in a relative clause, where subjects or direct objects are relativised; it is optional, when the head noun is in the dative or ablative case; and it is obligatory when the head noun is in the locative, benefactive or instrumental case.

This observation partly supports Keenan's generalisation (1985:147), where it is claimed that if the head noun is the non-direct object or the object of a postposition, it is more common to find it expressed by a personal pronoun. On the other hand, it is not common for the subject and direct object to be expressed as a personal pronoun in the relative clause. However, the behaviour of the dative and ablative cases is different from the locative, benefactive, and instrumental cases. In other words, although the head noun in the dative or ablative case is a non-direct object, its personal pronoun can be unexpressedin the relative clause.

Keenan (1985:148) further states that retaining personal pronouns in the NP position of the relative clause is very rare in head-final relative clauses, and he mentions Mandarin as the only counter-example. However, as we see in the following sentences, Azeri is also a counter-example to this generalisation; that is, when the head noun is in the locative, benefactive or instrumental case, it can occur as a pronoun in a head-final relative clause:

97 (a) män bag -da gal -dI -m

I garden -LOC stay -PAST -1SG

'I stayed in the garden.'

(b) män or-da gal -yan bag

I there -LOC stay -REL garden

'the garden where I stayed'

98 (a) män kiši -ichin oxu -

du -m I man -BEN

sing -PAST -1SG 'I

sang for the man.'

(b) män on -uchun oxu

-yan kiši I 3SG -BEN

sing -REL

man 'the man whom I sang for'

99 (a) män mIdad -Inan
yaz -dI -m I
pencil -INST write -PAST -
1SG 'I wrote with the pencil.'
(b) män on -unan yaz -dIg -Im
mId
adI 3SG -INST write -REL -POSS.1SG
pencil 'the pencil which I wrote with'

The occurrence of the head noun as a pronoun in the relative clause is only possible for locative, benefactive and instrumental cases.

3.2.2.2.4 **Headless relative clauses**

In Azeri, a relative clause can occur without the head; that is, it is possible to delete the head of a relative clause. The following examples illustrate headless relative clauses with the head being in different cases:

(A) **Nominative case**

100 (a) alma yey -yän kiši get -di
apple eat -REL man (NOM) go -PAST.3SG

'The man who was eating the apple went.'

(b) alma yey -yän get -di

apple eat -REL go -PAST.3SG

'(Someone) who was eating the apple went.'

101 (a) män gör -düg -üm kiši get -di

I see -REL -POSS.1SG man (NOM) go -PAST.3SG

'The man whom I saw went.'

(b) män gör -düg -üm get -di

I see -REL -POSS.1SG go -PAST.3SG

'(Someone) whom I saw went.'

(B) **Accusative case**

102 (a) män al -yan kitab -I gör -dü

I buy -REL book -ACC see -PAST.3SG

'He saw the book which I bought.'

(b) män al -yan -I gör -dü

I buy -REL -ACC see -PAST.3SG

'He saw (something) which I bought.'

103 (a) män al -dIg kita -I gör -dü
-Im b
I buy -REL - boo -ACC see -
POSS.1SG k PAST.3SG
'He saw the book which I bought.'

(b) män al -dIg -Im -I gör -dü

I buy -REL -POSS.1SG -ACC see -PAST.3SG

'He saw (something) which I bought.'

(C) **Dative case**

104 (a) män al -yan kitab -ya bax -dI
I buy -REL book -DAT look -PAST.3SG

'He looked at the book which I bought.'

(b) män al -yan -ya bax -dI

I buy -REL -DAT look -PAST.3SG

'He looked at (something) which I bought.'

105 (a) män al -dIg -Im kitab -ya bax -dI
I buy -REL -POSS.1SG book -DAT look -
PAST.3SG

'He looked at the book which I bought.'

(b) män al -dIg -Im -ya bax -dI

I buy -REL -POSS.1SG -DAT look -PAST.3SG

'He looked at (something) which I bought.'

(D) **Ablative case**

106 (a) män al -yan alma -dan yey -dI

I buy -REL apple -ABL eat -PAST.3SG

'He ate from the apple which I bought.'

(b) män al -yan -dan yey -dI

I buy -REL -ABL eat -PAST.3SG

'He ate from (something) which I bought.'

107 (a) män al -dIg -Im alma -dan yey -dI

I buy -REL -POSS.1SG apple -ABL eat -PAST.3SG

'He ate from the apple which I bought.'

(b) män al -dIg -Im -dan yey -dI

I buy -REL -POSS.1SG -ABL eat -PAST.3SG

'He ate from (something) which I bought.'

(E) **Instrumental case**

108 (a) män al -yan mIdad -Inan yaz -dI
I buy -REL pencil -INST write -PAST.3SG

'He wrote with the pencil which I bought.'

(b) män al -yan -Inan yaz -dI

I buy -REL -INST write -PAST.3SG

'He wrote with (something) which I bought.'

109 (a) män al -dIg -Im mIdad -Inan yaz -dI
I buy -REL -POSS.1SG pencil -INST write -PAST.3SG

'He wrote with the pencil which I bought.'

(b) män al -dIg -Im -Inan yaz -dI

I buy -REL -POSS.1SG -INST write -PAST.3SG

'He wrote with (something) which I bought.'

(F) **Benefactive case**

110 (a) män al -yan mIdad -IchIn gäz -di
I buy -REL pencil -BEN search-PAST.3SG

'He searched for the pencil which I bought.'

(b) män al -yan -IchIngäz -di

I buy -REL -BEN search -PAST.3SG

'He searched for (something) which I bought.'

111 (a) män al -dIg -Im mIdad -IchIn gäz -di

I buy -REL -POSS.1SG pencil -BEN search -PAST.3SG

'He searched for the pencil which I bought.'

(b) män al -dIg -Im -IchIn gäz -di

I buy -REL -POSS.1SG -BEN search -PAST.3SG

'He searched for (something) which I bought.'

There is a constraint on the deletion of the head in the relative clause. When the head is in the locative case, and the relativiser is /yAn/, it can not be deleted. However, when the relativiser is /dIg/, it can still be deleted:

112 (a) män al -yan kitab -dayaz -dI

I buy -REL book -LOC write -PAST.3SG

'He wrote in the book which I bought.'

(b) * män al -yan -da yaz -dI

I buy -REL -LOC write -PAST.3SG

113 (a) män al -dIg -Im kitab -da yaz -dI

I buy -REL -POSS.1SG book -LOC write -PAST.3SG

'He wrote in the book which I bought.'

(b) män al -dIg -Im -da yaz -dI

I buy -REL -POSS.1SG -LOC write -PAST.3SG

'He wrote in (something) which I bought.'

As we see in (112a), since the head, /kitab/ 'book', is in the locative case and the relativiser is /yAn/, its deletion results in the ungrammaticality of (112b); however, (113b) is still grammatical because the relativiser is /dIg/.

We may account for this constraint in terms of avoidance of ambiguity. As was mentioned in section 1.1.2.6, the suffix /yAn/ can also occur preceding the locative suffix,

/dA/, to denote the simultaneous occurrence of two different actions, as illustrated by the following example:

114 sän gäl -yän -dä män get -di -m
1SG(NOM) come -REL -LOC I go
-PAST -1SG 'I went when you came.'

If we delete the head of the relative clause which is in the locative case, the locative suffix, /dA/, is affixed to the relativiser, /yAn/, and the resulting structure becomes the same as in (114), i.e /gälyändä/, and hence it becomes ambiguous. Therefore, the constraint is applied to avoid such an ambiguity.

Bibliography

Abdullayev, A. J., A. Seyidov & A. Hasanov. 1972. *The current Azerbaijani language(Müasir Azerbaijan dili).* Bakl: Sintaksis

Aronoff, M. 1976. *Word formation in generative grammar*. Cambridge, MA: MIT Press Asher, R. E. (ed.). 1994. *The encyclopedia of language and linguistics*. V.1. Oxford: Pergamon Press.

Behzadi, A. A. 1991. *Dictionary of Azarbaijani names (Färhäng e namhay e zäban e Farsi).* Tabriz: Ark

Behzadi, B. 1989. *Azarbaijani-Persian dictionary (Färhäng e Azärbayjani-Farsi).* Tehran: Donya

Blake, B. J. 1994. *Case*. Cambridge: Cambridge University Press

Brown, E. K. & J. E. Miller 1980. *Syntax: A linguistic introduction to sentencestructure*. London: Hutchinson

Cafarov, S. 1970. *The current Azerbaijani language (Müasir Azerbaijan dili).* Baku:Maarif

Clark, E. V. 1978. Locationals: Existential, locative and possessive constructions. In: J. H. Greenberg (ed.). *Universals of human language*. V.4, 85-126. Stanford: StanfordUniversity Press

Comrie, B. 1981. *The languages of the Soviet Union*. Cambridge: Cambridge UniversityPress

Comrie, B (ed.). 1987. *The world's major languages*. London: Croom Helm

Comrie, B. 1989. *Language universals and linguistic typology*. Oxford: Basil BlackwellDavies, E. 1986. *The English imperative*. London: Croom Helm

Ershadi-Far, A. 1991. *The grammar of Azerbaijani (Azärbayjan dilinin grameri).* Tabriz: Talash

Farzane, M. A. 1992. *The fundamentals of the grammar of Azarbaijani (Mäbani edästur e zäban e Azärbayjani).* Tabriz: Farhang

Fraenkel, G. 1962. *A generative grammar of Azerbaijani*. Ph D thesis. Indiana University

Grimes, B. F. (ed.). 1992. *Ethnologue: languages of the world* (12th edition). Texas:Summer Institute of Linguistics

Hasanov, G. , K. Aliyov & F. Jalilov. 1991. *The grammar of the language ofAzerbaijan*. Tabriz: Talash

Householder, F. V & M. Lotfi. 1961. *Basic course in Azerbaijani*. The Hague: Mouton Katz, J. J. & P. M. Postal. 1964. *An integrated theory of linguistic descriptions*. Cambridge, MA: MIT

Katzner, K. 1986. *The languages of the world*. London: Routledge and Kegan Paul Keenan, E. L. 1985. Relative clauses In: T. Shopen (ed.) *Language typology and syntactic description*, V. 1, 243-281. Cambridge: Cambridge University Press Kornfilt, J. 1987. Turkish and the Turkic languages. In: B. Comrie (ed.). *The world's major languages*, 619-644. London: Croom Helm

Lee, S. N. 1996. *A grammar of Iranian Azerbaijani*. Unpublished Ph. D thesis. Sussex University.

Noonan, M. 1985. Complementation. In: T. Shopen. *Language typology and syntacticdescription*, V 2, 42-140. Cambridge: Cambridge University Press

Palmer, F. R. 1986. *Mood and modality*. Cambridge: Cambridge University Press

Payne, J. R. 1985. Complex phrases and complex sentences. In: T. Shopen (ed.).

Language typology and syntactic description, V 2, 3-41

Payne, T. E. 1997. *Describing morphosyntax: a guide for field linguists*. Cambridge: Cambridge University Press

Pir-Hashemi, T. 1990. *The grammar of Azary Turki (Dästur e zäban e Torki e Azäri)*.

Tabriz: Tabriz University Press

Rafraf, E. 1995. *Lessons in Azarbaijani (Ana dili: Azärbajjanja därslik)*. Tehran: Murghe Amin

Sadock, M. J & A. M. Zwicky. 1985. Speech act distinctions in syntax. In: T. Shopen (ed.). *Language typology and syntactic description*, V1, 155-196. Cambridge: Cambridge University Press

SBS. 1995. *SBS World Guide*. Melbourne: Reed Reference Australia

Stockwell, R. P., P. Schachter & B. H. Partee. 1971. *The major syntactic structures of English*. New York: Holt, Rinehart and Winston

Thorne, J. P. 1966. English imperative sentences. *Journal of Linguistics*, 2, 69-78 Underhill, R. 1976. *Turkish grammar*. Cambridge, MA: MIT Press.

Windfuhr, G. L. 1979. *Persian grammar: history and state of its study*. The Hague: Mouton

Yusifov, Y, B. 1987. On the significance of old toponyms in the study of the ethic history of Azerbaijan. *Izvestiya Akademii Nauk Azerbaidzhanskoi SSR, Literatura, yazyk I iskusstvo*, 2, 101-110

Zehtabi, M. T. 1991. *Current literary Azeri (Müasir ädäbi Azäri dili)*. Tabriz: Eldar

About the Author

Dr. Yavar Dehghani is a linguist, translator, interpreter, and educator with over two decades of experience in language research, teaching, and professional practice. He holds a PhD in Linguistics from La Trobe University, Melbourne, Australia, where his doctoral research focused on a comparative analysis of the grammatical structures of Azeri, Turkish, English, and Persian — the scholarly foundation from which the present volume emerges.

Dr. Dehghani is an accredited translator and interpreter with the National Accreditation Authority for Translators and Interpreters (NAATI), working across Persian, Azeri, and English. His professional work spans a wide range of settings, reflecting both his deep linguistic expertise and his commitment to bridging language and cultural barriers in practical, real-world contexts.

As a prolific author and self-publisher, Dr. Dehghani has produced an extensive catalogue of titles covering language learning, cultural guides, mindfulness, wisdom traditionsbooks across multiple languages including Persian, Dari, Azerbaijani, Pashto, Turkish, and English.

Rooted in Iranian and broader Middle Eastern culture and language, Dr. Dehghani brings to his scholarly and creative work a rare combination of academic rigour, multicultural perspective, and genuine passion for the languages he studies and teaches.

www.ingramcontent.com/pod-product-compliance
Lightning Source LLC
LaVergne TN
LVHW031342150826
845673LV00009B/2831
9781537292618